SUNDOWN LEGENDS

ALSO BY MICHAEL CHECCHIO

A Clean, Well-Lighted Stream

SUNDOWN

A JOURNEY INTO THE AMERICAN SOUTHWEST

LEGENDS

MICHAEL CHECCHIO

ST. MARTIN'S PRESS ✿ NEW YORK

THOMAS DUNNE BOOKS.
An imprint of St. Martin's Press.

SUNDOWN LEGENDS: A JOURNEY INTO THE AMERICAN SOUTHWEST. Copyright ©
2000 by Michael Checchio. All rights reserved. Printed in the United States of
America. No part of this book may be used or reproduced in any manner whatsoever without written permission except in the case of brief quotations embod-
ied in critical articles or reviews. For information, address St. Martin's Press, 175
Fifth Avenue, New York, N.Y. 10010.

ISBN 0-312-20593-7

Book design by Michelle McMillian
Frontispiece by Photodisc Inc.

First Edition: April 2000

10 9 8 7 6 5 4 3 2 1

CONTENTS

Prologue   1

1. Into the Light   7

2. The Great Abyss   13

3. Up on the Rim   24

4. Canyon Shangri-la   32

5. A Grand Staircase   44

6. Sundown Legend   55

7. Uncharted Terrain   68

8. A Wrinkle in the Earth   77

9. Rimrock World   86

10. Slickrock Capital   93

11. A Walk in the Desert   104

12. Indian Country   111

13. Breath Spirits   129

14. Canyon of Death   137

15. Ghosts   149

16. Trout Fishing in New Mexico   157

17. From the Faraway Nearby   167

18. Santa Fake   173

19. The Way to Taos   183

20. Magical Realism   204

21. Spirit Country   217

SUNDOWN LEGENDS

PROLOGUE

Point Imperial ... North Rim, Grand Canyon.

False dawn ... The last stars blinking over the desert ... 43°F and climbing ... humidity low ... barometer rising.

Stars fading ... A subtle shifting to gray on the eastern horizon ... Dim outline of canyon rim ... a sunken darkness awaiting below.

Gray all around now ... Cliff walls forming out of a flat backdrop ... The sun preparing to come up over the Painted Desert ...

Sky reddening in the east.

A reddish glow behind the formation known as Palisades of the Desert. A curtain of red hanging on the east. Clouds taking on color, trimmed in blues and coral pinks. The canyon deepening and taking on shape.

On the horizon, the momentary appearance of the uppermost part of the sun's disk ... Light bends at the moment of sunrise, the reds in the spectrum suppressed, the blues dispersed into the great dome of atmosphere.

A flash of yellow on the eastern horizon. Daybreak.

A fireball rises over the Painted Desert and the day begins. A globe of flaming hydrogen rising above the horizon. The desert submits to the glory of the rising sun. The eastern sky is blue and pink. Shadows spread and the canyon gloom draws downward. Rimrock walls become visible, take on form.

Revealed—the Painted Desert stretching away to the east . . . Marble Canyon to the north . . . the Coconino Plateau to the south . . . And the abyss that separates it all . . . Barely visible across the wide canyon, the dim trench of the Little Colorado . . . Sunlight fires the Vermilion Cliffs, their rosy buttes flushed with light. . . . The canyon rimrock facing the east brightens into a sunlit band . . . and the ravines below this strip of light take on pearl-gray halftones. . . . Daylight shines on the Marble Platform, flat as a billiard table . . . on Navajo Mountain, a distant outline rising in Utah . . . on the mesas of the Hopi Reservation, dimly coming into view. . . . The tip of Mount Hayden in the canyon glows in new sunlight. . . . Visible far across the rim is the top of Mount Humphrey and the other San Francisco Peaks.

The light is filling the abyss of the Grand Canyon. . . . The canyon seems to deepen, its alcoves receding into the rock walls. . . . Time and scale are altered in its vast yawn. . . . The view is numbing. . . . Bright bands of rimrock take on color and tone as sunlight crawls down the canyon wall.

The view is open and perfect. . . . Distances in the Painted Desert run out endlessly. . . . The sky turns blue and gold. . . . The light is cleanly transparent, a golden fire toward the sun, a deep hazy blue in the canyon depths. . . . A world of rock is beginning to warm. . . .

Eddies of wind . . . clouds . . . stillness.

THAT'S THE WAY the sun came up on the morning of June 3, 1998, as I saw it from Point Imperial, highest overlook on the

Grand Canyon. Just another Grand Canyon sunrise. Just one more dawn.

I had an entire month before me to spend in the desert Southwest. Two days before, I had rented a four-wheel-drive sports utility vehicle and had left my home in northern California. Laden with camping gear, I headed for the outback. In the desert, you have the familiar yet alien feeling that you are on the brink of everything and nothing. In the desert, you are in the presence of something you can't quite name.

My plan, largely unformed, was to explore the redrock canyon lands of Arizona and Utah—to do a rough approximation of what is sometimes called the "Grand Circle of the Colorado Plateau." And then to head for the uplands of New Mexico. To travel without purpose or fixed itinerary. To go where mood and interest took me. Tonight, I would be camping on the North Rim of the Grand Canyon, sleeping under the swaying pines high up on the Kaibab Plateau. I would descend into canyons, see Indian reservations, hike the redrock country, and follow Jeep trails into sun-blasted deserts. I would revisit old haunts and explore new ones—and in so doing rediscover a world I thought I already knew.

I MAKE MY home in San Francisco, where almost daily I can hear the sound of foghorns. But the desert is only half a day's drive from this city of moist salt winds and barking sea lions. Traveling eastward from my wet redwood coast, across the very dull Central Valley, and up into the Sierra Nevada, one comes to the roof of California. From this high escarpment, the drop-off is one of the steepest and most spectacular descents on the planet. Below lies an American outback, a great rain shadow, spreading all the way to the Rocky Mountains. The Great Basin and northern Mojave deserts converge here beneath the wall of California. Here is Mono Lake, a saline inland sea, one of the world's oldest and most surreal bodies of water. To the east are the White and Inyo mountains and behind them the void of the Nevada desert. High on the slopes of the Whites and Inyos grow the twisted trunks of bristlecone pines, the longest continuously living life-forms on earth, alive as seedlings at the time of Moses. In only a matter of miles, the topography changes from subalpine meadows to sagebrush scrub. Here are blistering deserts and cooling pine forests and towering crags hung with glaciers. A landscape of sagebrush, lava fields, cinder cones, fault scarps, and ancient alkali flats, contrasted with narrow ribbons of wetland, subalpine forests, quaking aspen, and shimmering trout waters. A land so dramatic and infinitely varied and underpopulated, many of us wonder why it was never made into a national park.

My travels in the eastern Sierra Nevada would take me into desert outposts with names like Tom's Place, Lee Vining, and Lone Pine. At night, these small towns looked like dusty jewelry in the empty blackness of the desert night. The drive might take me into mountains with blue alpine lakes or down into long shadow valleys with their eerie atmospheric convections and summer lightning strikes. I made it a point to drive out to Manzanar, the California concentration camp where Japanese-Americans were interned during World War II. Another time, I visited Bodie, the largest intact ghost town in the West, with students' papers still lying atop school desks, glasses set up on bars, apothecary bottles filling drugstore windows—as if the residents had simply decided to pull up stakes and flee en masse.

Heartbreaking and exhilarating battles were fought over this land. In the first half of the twentieth century, the city of Los Angeles managed an imperialist seizure of the water in the Owens Valley. (That long-ago theft was memorialized in the film *Chinatown*.) Conservationists such as Mary Austin (*The*

Land of Little Rain) and Ansel Adams decried the drying up of a once-lush river valley that supported orchards and well-irrigated ranches. I used to believe as they did, that it was a tragedy of inestimable proportions. But now I had come to believe that maybe it was also a blessing in disguise. With most of the water in the Owens River siphoned off to Los Angeles, three hundred miles away, there had been little opportunity for the kind of agricultural and real estate development that would have transformed this desert region into another San Fernando Valley.

The road south from Mono Lake and the Owens Valley leads to the lowest sink in the United States, Death Valley. In the winter of 1998, California was battered by the wettest El Niño in recorded history. The result was a riot of wildflowers in Death Valley. No one had seen anything like it in decades. Seeds that had been dormant for more than twenty years split open, bringing life and color to the desert. Miles of wildflowers carpeted Death Valley. CBS dispatched a film crew to broadcast the bright fields of color to the nation.

Once considered useless, the Southern California desert, fully a third of the state, was now thought worthy of some degree of protection. In a single sweeping bill known as the California Desert Protection Act of 1994, Congress created a patchwork of more than 9 million acres of federal park and wilderness land, all assembled out of huge chunks of the Mojave.

The Mojave resembles the Big Nothing. Seen from the road, it is America's dullest and most featureless desert. It doesn't have any of those giant cacti the color of fresh-cut limes that you find in the Sonoran Desert of southern Arizona. Nor does it have the Great Basin's fragrant sagebrush vistas, more changeable in color and tone than the ocean. Nor sunsets as melodramatic as those that fall on the purple buttes and pink canyons of the Colorado Plateau. But the Mojave is the kind of place that could produce a new faith. When the thunder rumbles over the mountains, one could almost believe that a prophecy is about to be handed down.

It is no surprise that three of the world's great religions came out of a desert. In the desert, a person can feel both inconsequential and important at the same time. Left alone in such a terrain, one either comes alive or folds in the face of so much harshness. The desolation and silence of the desert are filled with psychic dangers. Here is the universe as other.

In the Mojave, the driest desert in the United States, Joshua trees—named after the successor of Moses who raised his arms to God—stand as if beseeching the sky for rain. This is a place of contrasts. Harshness and delicacy, stillness and booming sound, bright light and isolation. A world of sand and rock and spiky plants, where the days can be unbearably hot, the nights freezing, and where the animals don't so much survive as blend into the barrenness. Jackrabbits and kangaroo rats, burros and coyotes, tarantulas and rattlesnakes live out here, and not much else. Certainly not many human beings, and for good reason. But something is out here. That much is certain.

Night in the desert. Far away a coyote yips. Owls hoot in the darkness. Observe the moon rising over the Joshua trees. Listen to the desert. The desert is trying to tell you something. When the desert speaks, you have to listen. And what is the desert trying to say? I couldn't tell you. I'm only talking to myself, and right now, the whole world is answering.

1

INTO THE LIGHT

I HAD BEEN studying the maps all winter. Reading the names on the printed page and responding to their power and mystery: Cape Royal, Dirty Devil River, the Maze, Shiprock, Hovenweep, Canyon del Muerto, Moenkopi, Keet Seel, Desolation Canyon, Dead Horse Point. I savored those names in my mind. They had deep meaning and a mythic association.

I had cabin fever, if one can be said to have cabin fever in San Francisco. I needed to get out of town. Needed to sort out my camping gear and get back to nature—whatever that means. Experience some of the freshness and cleanliness of the physical world. Maybe I could swing a trip to the Grand Canyon and Utah. See Navajoland again. Fish for trout in New Mexico, a state I had never visited, despite the fact that two of my sisters were now living there. The weather would probably be at its best in late May and early June. The desert flowers would still be in bloom. I would get to see the Maze and the Land of Standing Rocks again. Fly-fish in the San Juan River. Visit the Waterpocket Fold and the Grand Staircase. Maybe even get up to Mesa Verde in Colorado. Camp out, hike, explore. Maybe buy a day's glimpse back into Eden. Experience the original, lost conditions.

My goal, my general destination, was the Colorado Plateau, the famous redrock region that lies between the Rocky Mountains and the Mojave and Great Basin deserts. That was the heart of the American Southwest, I felt, that fantastic land formed by the Colorado River and its tributaries. I wanted to see those rivers again, flowing like golden taffy down in their desiccated canyons. It had been a while since I was last out there, but I had never forgotten those salmon pink tablelands and azure skies filled with ravens.

I can't say for sure exactly what I meant to find on my road trip. Perhaps travel down that ancient corridor, back into a world that had made us what we are today. Discover levels of myself that were deeper than the ordinary self.

Fashionable male therapy has it that we might begin to cure our psychic ills if only we can find a way to reconnect to the primitive man within. Now, I wasn't about to give up my morning copy of the *New York Times* or any of the other amenities of civilization. But I think I know what the drum beaters were getting at. Modern man needed to be restored to his original self. I needed restoration, too.

ON THE FIRST of June, the morning of my departure, I rented a Chevy Blazer, and the rental agent made a very big deal about warning me not to take it off the paved road. Now, there was a rule not likely to be obeyed. What did these fools think four-wheel drive had been invented for? I was heading for the end of the pavement. I needed an off-road escape vehicle to take me where I wanted to go in an up-and-down landscape of mountains, high deserts, and canyons. I didn't much like the Chevy Blazer. You didn't drive it—it drove you. Everything was automated—you couldn't crack open a window without having to switch on the power. What would happen if I rolled the car down an embankment, into a river, and the water shorted out the electrical system and I couldn't open the window to escape? I wanted to ask the rental agent what I should do in such an emergency, but I thought it best not to tip him off to my intentions. Didn't want him getting suspicious and canceling the rental agreement. What he didn't know wouldn't hurt him. Normally, I don't approve of SUVs, which are more like armored personnel carriers than cars, and totally unnecessary on paved roads. But I was going to need the Blazer's low gears and high-suspension clearance. And unless I did something very foolish, like demolish the undercarriage on a Jeep trail blazed by a uranium miner, the rental agency folks would be none the wiser. The truth is, I don't much like cars. Haven't washed one since I was a teenager. All I ask is that a car be reliable. And I knew my eleven-year-old Honda Civic, my faithful city car, wasn't suitable for going off-road in canyon country.

I packed my camping gear into the Blazer, and in the late morning of June 1, 1998, laden with enough provisions to last a month, I headed off alone for the North Rim of the Grand Canyon.

The Mojave, the Big Nowhere, America's driest and most boring desert, at least the part that is seen from the highway, began to show itself east of the Central Valley hub town of Bakersfield. I hate driving in the Central Valley. It is the dullest and least cheerful thing there is about California. Driving the length of the Central Valley is a sentence in purgatory. You feel as if the valley will never run out. Only man could create a landscape this dismal and depressing. Once a beautiful savanna filled with native grasses, it was now all mechanized farms, the world's largest industrial park, a terrain completely altered and wholly given over to the service of agribusiness. Where once tule elk and pronghorn antelope grazed the Central Valley in herds, now there were only crop-dusted fields and roads cutting up the checkerboard flatness. The wind scattered dust and pesticides everywhere. You couldn't see the Sierra Nevada for the smog. I drove on an interstate alongside Teamster-driven double-trailer convoys discharging more smudge into the atmosphere. And the waste! Aqueducts and canals evaporating in the heat. Pump pistons banging along the rivers. Snakelike siphons spraying into endless rows of crops. Factory silos and barns the size of blimp hangars rose like mirages off the hot, shimmering rectangles of cropland. Each ag town was more dreary than the last. The only good thing that ever came out of Bakersfield was Merle Haggard. It was terribly hot when I arrived at that god-awful bleak town, as it always is in Bakersfield in summertime, and the heat only got worse after I crossed the Tehachapis.

A golden radiance of late afternoon fell on the Tehachapi Mountains. But I had no plans to linger in the Mojave. Outside of the desert town of Barstow, I joined the Southern California traffic stream bound for Las Vegas. Although I was doing eighty, other drivers were hurtling past, in a rush to lose their money. Why does everyone in America seem to want to go to Vegas? The sun began to set behind me in a brilliant band of light. Sable shadows stretched across the sands of the Mojave until all the shadows finally combined to darken the desert world and turn it into night. Ahead was emptiness and a lonely pitch-blackness. And then in the distance, unimaginably far away, a tiny glint appeared on the black desert. A tray of jewelry on black velvet. Stateline, Nevada, a small town with a huge electric bill.

I drove past Stateline—its outsized fun-house casinos garishly lit up by neon—and back into the empty sea of darkness. Casino gambling had created Stateline out of the nothingness of the desert—it was for those sorry Californians too impatient to drive all the way to Vegas. Only the most desperate gambler must wind up in such a bunghole. The blackness continued for a long time. And then another glittering jewel appeared far, far away in the night. This light beckoned, and it just kept growing and growing, getting bigger and bigger, and it wouldn't stop growing, becoming a great vast glitter fire in the desert.

I roared into Las Vegas, a city born out of boredom and desperation. Las Vegas was invented as the antidote to the nation's tedium, but in reality, it had done very little to relieve dull minds. The approach to Vegas was lined with neon commercials, most of them offering free buffets. The casino architecture wasn't so much tasteless as it was a parody of bad taste. New York's skyline was lit up as if for a Broadway revue and an Egyptian pyramid arose before me like something off the set of *Aida*. One attraction was even disguised as a pirate ship, as if to remind us that nothing so hilarious could possibly be all that bad for us. The streets were full of noise and honk and people trying much too hard to have fun. The inside of a casino is a curiously unjoyous place. You get the feeling that the gamblers would be just as happy if someone hit them on the back of the head with a sap. Gambling might be just another form of entertainment, as its boosters insist, but very few people go out into the parking lot and shoot themselves after seeing a movie. Still, any town created by the likes of Bugsy Siegel can't be viewed entirely as a bad thing. Las Vegas is for people who like to totter on the edge of spectacular failures, and more than a few people have been known to ruin their lives with the special compulsions this town breeds. But it could be argued that some people are just prone to screwing things up anyway, and it is easy to imagine them wrecking their lives even without the added inducements of gambling. I, for one, used to live and work in Atlantic City, and I know how to have a good time in a casino. The trick is to not spend any money and just watch the other people.

I left Las Vegas early the next morning, not wanting to linger in a place where Wayne Newton is considered the most popular entertainer. By rights, Las Vegas shouldn't exist at all. Las Vegas is a miracle in the desert. A million people live in a place that doesn't have its own natural water supply. And more are coming to live here all the time. The secret to its success lies on the other side of those drab desert hills called the Muddy Mountains. There sits the cesspit of Lake Mead, the Colorado River plugged up by Hoover Dam. Las Vegas is already using more than its fair allotment of Colorado River water—water it has to share with the rest of the Southwest, which includes Southern California—and yet it has no plans whatsoever to curb its growth. The funniest thing about Las Vegas is that the city invented by Bugsy Siegel and the mob is now trying to promote itself as a family resort. I thought of all those kids abandoned at the hotel arcades while their parents went off to roll dice or pull the arms on slot machines. Las Vegas seems laughable, quite harmless really, until you realize that the clouds of mustard gas hanging over the basin as smog eventually drift their way over to the Grand Canyon, spoiling the views on some days. Then the idea of Las Vegas becomes a little like Bugsy Siegel himself, criminal and stupid.

2

THE GREAT ABYSS

THE DESERT WAS covered with creosote bushes and Joshua trees shaped like slingshots. I was still in the dry and charmless Mojave, but on its northern borderland, between high desert and redrock plateau. I followed the highway out of the monotonous Mojave until I left Nevada, entering Arizona through a redrock corridor that cut its way through the Virgin River Gorge. Now things were getting interesting. The walls of the canyon were reddish and streaked with black desert varnish. Following the river canyon for about forty miles, I managed to cross the extreme northwestern corner of Arizona and pass into Utah. Soon I found myself at St. George, a rapidly growing Mormon retirement community in the redrock desert. A few miles beyond and I was driving through Hurricane, a town that never saw one. Here I turned south onto a narrow road that led back across the Arizona state line again and into the backcountry known as the Arizona Strip.

The Arizona Strip had pretty much remained a no-man's-land well into the twentieth century. Although related to Utah geographically and culturally, both Utah and Arizona once laid claim to it. Mormon settlers ranched the area, and their herds of sheep, cattle, and horses grazed on remote meadows near the North Rim of the Grand Canyon. Deer herds in the pine forests attracted occasional sportsmen. One sport who kept coming back was President Theodore Roosevelt, who established a federal game reserve there. As statehood was under debate, Sharlot Hall, a historian and chronicler of the Arizona Territory, mounted her own expedition across the Strip. Her lectures and published articles convinced many of the value of the region, and it was included within the borders when Arizona finally became a state in 1912.

And yet it remained remote. When Grand Canyon National Park was finally established in 1919, most of the park's acreage lay on the north side of the canyon. And yet the northern rim remained virtually inaccessible to tourists. Any visitor on the South Rim trying to get to the North Rim by automobile had a perilous passage. The road was bad and automobiles often got stuck. The river crossing at Lees Ferry was tricky. It was better to go around to the west through Nevada. The road was slightly better, and it took only a mere week to ten days to get to the North Rim.

Today, some of that original feeling of remoteness remains. The North Rim of the Grand Canyon is still, as folks like to say, "a long way on a dead-end road." Noise and overcrowding has not yet ruined the good side of the Grand Canyon. Of course, that is changing. Word is getting out.

Immediately upon recrossing the state line, I drove into the tiny Arizona community of Colorado City. This extreme northwestern corner of Arizona, cut off from the rest of the state by the Grand Canyon, was sometimes called the "Mormon Dixie." The flyspeck town of Colorado City was founded in the 1930s by renegade Mormons seeking to carry on their grand tradition of polygamy. Even today, Colorado City, like much of the Arizona Strip, remains one of the nation's last bastions for polyg-amy. In 1890, facing military and legal threats, such as forfeiture of church property by the federal government, the Mormon Church in Salt Lake City officially abandoned its practice of plural marriage and backed up its order with a threat to ex-communicate all polygamists. Many polygamists fled Utah for northwestern Arizona. Beyond the reach of Mormon law in Utah, and cut off from the rest of Arizona by the Grand Canyon, the renegade Mormons thought no authority would touch them, much less care about them. How wrong they were. During much of this century, the dissenters found themselves the victims of raids, roundups, and general harassment. Per-haps the most truly oppressive raid took place in Colorado City in 1953, when authorities arrested 26 men and ordered 253 chil-dren placed into foster care. A few of the kids weren't even Mormons, but they were collared anyway in all the confusion. It took years to get the mess straightened out.

I have never understood the prejudice against polygamy in our time. Or rather, I understand it all too clearly but can't justify it. I suspect that one day soon the United States Supreme Court will be forced to revisit its landmark ruling on the sub-ject. The idea of what constitutes a family today has changed radically from what it was when the Supreme Court outlawed polygamy in the late nineteenth century. In that ruling, the high court determined that freedom of religion was not an absolute and did not extend to violations of public morality. But public morality wore a much different mask then than it does today. In our time, when it's common for so many children to be raised by only one parent, it's hard to argue that children with three or more parents are somehow disadvantaged. And any-way, a majority of modern Americans already practice plural marriage, at least serially.

The Arizona Strip is still a great place to hide out. It comprises four huge plateaus—8,400 square miles of wilderness—with only four tiny towns. Imagine a chunk of real estate the size of Delaware, Connecticut, and Rhode Island combined, with only two paved roads. Fewer than four thousand people live on the Arizona Strip. It belongs mostly to us, the public, and is managed largely by federal agencies—namely, the Bureau of Land Management, the Forest Service, and the National Park Service. With poor roads, it is cut off to the east and the south by the great trench of the Grand Canyon, and to the west by Kanab Canyon. Timber and ranching are mainstays, but there is very little private property. Very little water, too, only a few precious springs, like Pipe Spring on the Kaibab-Paiute Indian Reservation. You can hike the canyons and brave the Jeep trails, but you had better not break down in the backcountry. Especially in the badlands west of Kanab Canyon, where there isn't a single paved road. You might not see another Jeep for days.

The road to the Grand Canyon wends its way through space and silence. In the western distances, across the vastness of the plateau country, I could make out what I took to be the outlines of the Grand Wash Cliffs. On my immediate left, much closer, was a flaring escarpment of red buttes known as the Vermilion Cliffs. The red-and-pink cliffs seemed to be ignited from within by their own inner light. The Vermilion Cliffs mark the southern edge of the Paria Plateau; they end at Lees Ferry, where the Grand Canyon begins.

A dirt road veering abruptly to the right led to Pipe Spring, but I ignored this turnoff. I was eager to get to the Grand Canyon. At the little community of Fredonia, the road veered south again and began to climb into the pines and grassy meadows of the Kaibab Plateau. I stopped to refuel at a crossroads gas station at Jacob Lake and then continued on my way down the road that I knew would dead-end at the Grand Canyon's

North Rim. The elevation had been rising dramatically all the while. The densely forested country opened up in spots onto high montane meadows known as parks. These were edged in thick stands of pine and spruce. The air was cool and sweet despite an awful desert heat that surely would be awaiting below in the depths of the Grand Canyon. There were plenty of aspens up here, great stands of white-barked trees; their leaves splashed a light springtime luminescence. Lupine and New Mexican locust bloomed in the meadows. This North Rim of the Grand Canyon, a full thousand feet higher than its sister rim, was cooler and moister, its plateau covered in a thick forest of ponderosa pine, white and Douglas fir, blue and Engelmann spruce, and quaking aspens.

I passed in and out of pine forests and bowl-shaped meadows and glades of shivering aspens. Patches of old snow lay on the ground, especially in areas that seemed to be in permanent shade. The white-barked aspens were newly leafing out, creating a shimmering canopy of greenish gold above the forest floor. I thought what lovely trout country this must make. But there were no brooks or streams up on the Kaibab Plateau. The Kaibab limestone—the porous rock that formed the uppermost layer of the Grand Canyon's rim—absorbed all the rainfall and snowmelt. There was water, all right, collected in underground caverns deep in the rimrock. You could be hiking down in the Grand Canyon and find water gushing cold and pure out of springs or trickling from seeps in the rock wall.

The southern Paiute, who hunted deer on this forest plateau, named it Kaibab—Mountain Lying Down. Winters are colder and wetter up here than on the lower South Rim. Because of heavier snowfall, the North Rim remains closed to visitors from mid-October to mid-May. (Cross-country skiers are allowed to schuss in, but snowmobiles are outlawed. There are no services in wintertime.)

I noticed dirt lanes branching off and disappearing into the pines. These lanes led through miles of wild timber until coming out abruptly onto dramatic viewpoints on the rim of the Grand Canyon, some overlooking House Rock Valley and the Marble Platform. It was permissible to camp for free outside the park boundary within the national forest, a good thing to keep in mind when the campgrounds in the park are filled up. There were any number of places to pitch a tent, well out of sight of a paved road, at the edges of splendid meadows, or under shady pines and rustling aspens. Just outside of the entrance to the park, I spotted the dirt road that veers off to the right toward Point Sublime, twenty-three miles away on the canyon rim. Few tourists make it to Point Sublime because the road is impossible, if not outright impassable. Only a sturdy Jeep-type vehicle with a high clearance could get you through. This year, I would try to make it to what many consider to be the most magnificent overlook on the Grand Canyon.

But first things first. I had booked myself in advance into the North Rim campground for two nights, and I needed to secure my campsite. Visitors are warned to make their reservations months in advance; I had made mine only the week before, and somehow I had gotten a site. The weather might have had something to do with it. At the park entrance, I asked the ranger manning the tollbooth how cold temperatures were getting at night. He said the mercury had dropped to 33°F the previous night. Blame El Niño.

"When the park opened," the ranger said, "we still had a lot of snow on the ground." Ah, here was the reason I had managed to book the campsite so easily.

It was early June, and there were still a few scattered snowdrifts and surviving dunes of old snow lying around. The afternoon was warm and smelled of sunshine and fresh pine scents. El Niño rains had pushed springtime back a month. I could expect to enjoy May-like weather all through June, and thus escape much of the terrible heat of the desert in high summer. But it was going to be bitterly cold up here on the North Rim after nightfall.

A trip to the Grand Canyon isn't exactly a meditative journey of solitude. In summer, the South Rim, the side of the canyon that receives the bulk of 5 million visitors annually, can resemble a bad toupee. But the North Rim is the connoisseur's side of the Grand Canyon. Few people manage both rims on a single visit. The canyon is only twelve miles across from rim to rim at its widest, but a five-hour, 216-mile journey by car. I had taken the trouble of coming in by the back door, and it was well worth the effort.

I pitched my tent and set up a hasty camp. And then I drove over to the Grand Canyon Lodge to orient myself to the view. Walking the bridle path along a side canyon, toward Bright Angel Point, I could hear but not see Roaring Springs, 3,800 feet below the rim, far down in the tributary canyon. Roaring Springs bursts out of the rocks above the sedimentary layer known as the Bright Angel shale. It is the only source of drinking water on the North Rim, and it is the most delicious water I have ever tasted. In the campground, my first order of business had been to dump the off-tasting Frisco and Vegas waters from my three canteens and fill them with the cold, clear goodness of the North Rim.

It's only a short walk from the lodge to Bright Angel Point— a quarter of a mile out onto a jutting peninsula of rock—but suddenly the cool green forest of the Kaibab Plateau gives way to stunted piñons and junipers. On flat land, you would have to travel several hundred miles before experiencing this kind of change, but the Grand Canyon compresses the transition from conifer forest to desert into a few hundred yards. The hot breath of the abyss rose up into my face. From the snow-covered top of Mount Humphrey, tallest of the San Francisco Peaks, as seen across the South Rim, sixty-five miles away, down to the burning furnace on the floor of the Grand Canyon, the traveler encounters as many life zones as on a five-thousand-mile journey from northern Canada to southern Mexico.

Well, here it was, the Grand Canyon, the standard by which all other great wonders of the earth are measured. I stared dumbfounded into it. And although I looked and gaped, I could not fully take it all in or even begin to comprehend it.

The extravagant light of Arizona emphasized the harsh perfection of the canyon. The palisade walls were stratified clearly as bands of brown, tan, orangish brown, orange-white, greenish brown, red, mauve, umber, pink, and ocher. Buttes and towers of rock, layered in the canyon's fiery colors, rose up out of an enormous chasm. Deva, Brahma, and Zoroaster temples stood as solid jutting masses, their buttes carved by erosion into fantastic forms. The temple monoliths had once been part of the North Rim, but time and erosion had separated them, leaving them lordly and isolate. I could hear Roaring Springs thousands of feet below me in the tributary canyon on my left. At my right, in Transept Canyon, I made out the wall of scarring where a massive section of Coconino sandstone had recently given way to gravity—a reminder that the bridge I was standing on at Bright Angel Point would one day be nothing but thin air. I gazed into the depths and contemplated the grandeur. Bright Angel Canyon descended southward out of view, disappearing along its fault line into the canyon folds. Lateral chasms cut into the Grand Canyon from all sides, receding far into its mass. Somewhere at the end of Bright Angel Canyon and the Kaibab foot trail was Phantom Ranch and beyond and below that the Colorado River carving out the inner gorge. But the river wasn't visible from anywhere up here on the point.

The banded palisades on the South Rim were eleven miles across the grand abyss. Ravens could cross it. The checkerspot butterfly, which lives on red blooms of Indian paintbrush on the canyon rims, could float easily across the vast expanse. I crossed it in my mind. Across that gulf, and sixty-five miles distant, rose the snow-capped San Francisco Peaks. A forest fire burning in the southern distance on the Coconino Plateau was spreading a faint haze across the canyon.

The Colorado River, a mile down and unseen from up here, had cut away and revealed the layers of the earth's age. The upper rock on which I stood, the layer of Kaibab limestone on the canyon rim, was only 200 million years old; the oldest rock exposed at the bottom of the gorge was 2 billion years of age. Over time, the river had cut downward while the rims thrust upward. The river even reversed directions once. The northern rim, on which I stood, was more than a thousand feet higher than the opposite rim, and much farther away from the river.

It was probably too late in the afternoon to drive out to Cape Royal. But I had time to see Point Imperial, the highest overlook in Grand Canyon National Park. I took the twisting road out through aspens and yellow pines to the magnificent overlook, almost nine thousand feet above sea level. Below the escarpment, glowing under an incandescent sky, stretching eastward toward dim blue mesas and volcanic peaks, was the Painted Desert. The desert below shimmered in the heat, as did the pinkish red buttes of the Vermilion Cliffs. But up here on Point Imperial, the air remained sparkling and cool. I stared into the narrow gorge of Marble Canyon and at the flat platform surrounding it. The Grand Canyon heads at Marble Gorge, the Colorado River cutting its way between the Vermilion and Echo cliffs. As seen from this height, the Marble Platform, spotted with juniper and piñon, and eroded by gullies, appeared as flat and even as a pool table. The vegetation was a soft olive green.

Toward the east, I made out the gorge of the Little Colorado, where it comes out of the Painted Desert and enters the Grand Canyon.

I watched the bluish shadows of clouds drifting over the Marble Platform and the Painted Desert. Gusty winds were spreading the faint haze from the forest fire that was burning far away on the Coconino Plateau. But I could still make out the dome of Navajo Mountain looming in the distance, a hundred miles away in Utah. The slopes of this mountain, sacred to the Navajo, apron off into the rock and sand of their sprawling reservation. The Navajo Reservation completely surrounds the smaller Hopi Reservation, whose three mesas I could see rising up on the far edge of the Painted Desert.

I returned to Bright Angel Point in time for the violet hour. Those folks not in camp preparing their suppers, or trying to get a table inside the Grand Canyon Lodge, were gathering on the point for the pink-and-mauve sundown. A golden illumination glowed on Red Butte, Brahma, Zoroaster, and Deva temples, and fired Angel's Gate, my favorite formation. The temple monoliths stood golden orange and furnace red in the final sundown. I stood for more than an hour on the point, watching the shifting play of light and shadow. Tone, color, and distance were abetted by the magic fall of light. You would think sunset and sunrise would simply be the reverse of each other, but this is not the case. The light of sunrise is cold; the light of sundown warm. Evenings linger longer than dawns. At dawn, everything is brilliant but indistinct. Evenings are flushed with a softer, gentler luminance. But both create an ambient truth and a supernal reality. The sun was setting on Grand Canyon and what was once grand had now become royal. All the details on the canyon walls were emerging. The summit band was a golden radiance, the strata below the lit-up rim rose and watermelon pink. Where the canyon dropped away into the depths below, rock and shadows were underlain with brooding hints of deeper color. The blaze of last sunlight pouring into the furnace canyon reflected back into the gulf and the air became a bluish and violet ether. Gradually, the sun sank and the colors in the canyon dimmed. And yet the western sky was filled with streamers of glory. As the sun disappeared behind the North Rim, the final light drained away and a blue sea filled the canyon. And from rim to rim, the canyon world was banked in deep purple shadowing. The lilac sky now turned to the darker grapiness of dusk and everything was flooded with a blue-and-purple majesty.

3

UP ON THE RIM

I RETURNED TO camp and wrote in my notebook by lantern light, expecting the muse to pee in my ear. But it got so cold, I could barely hold the pen in my hand, and so I crawled into the tent early.

The feeling of there being something out there absolutely unspoiled is a big part of the canyon's majesty. The Grand Canyon is more than just a sanctuary; it is life engaging us on older, deeper levels.

When you stand there looking into such a place, your senses become overwhelmed, but, conversely, you go into a more natural state. It's humbling and a little scary to confront such openness and space. The experience takes you out of your accustomed place in the universe and your insignificance hits you. You are merely one living creature, and your connection to the whole becomes that much clearer.

UP BEFORE DAWN in the blue-blackness to watch the sunrise at Point Imperial. Here was another major difference between sunrise and sunset: I was usually unconscious for the former.

Jesus, it was cold. I had tossed inside my sleeping bag all night, never quite warm enough. My neighbors, a group of college-age kids, had kept me up half the night with their off-key singing. I was much too cold to crawl out of my bag and tell them to shut the fuck up. I cursed myself for not having bought a mummy bag, but I had wanted the extra room of a rectangular sack, and I had figured that the weather would be mild enough to get away with it. I had figured wrong. Rectangular bags just don't retain heat like mummy sacks. I hoped this wasn't going to be a problem on my trip. Christ, the external thermometer in my Blazer was reading 38°F.

One of the college kids came over to borrow something (I forget exactly what, possibly a corkscrew), and he told me that he and his companions were on a circuit of all the national parks in the Southwest. The Grand Canyon was their first stop. His friends were slamming car doors, banging breakfast pots, and shouting at one another. But he seemed like a nice kid, and so I congratulated him on his choice of itinerary. "By the time you get to your last national park," I told him, "no doubt you'll have learned by then how to behave in a campground."

I drove out to Point Imperial, saw first light peeking out over the Painted Desert, and watched the curtain of a crimson-and-golden dawn rise up on the canyon world. From there, I took the winding road out to isolated Cape Royal to gaze upon the great stone monoliths of Wotans Throne and Vishnu Temple. Many of the monoliths in the Grand Canyon were named by the great nineteenth-century geologist Clarence Dutton, who accompanied Maj. John Wesley Powell on his second exploration of the Colorado River. Dutton's references to Hindu religion, Eastern mysticism, and Egyptology struck me as inappropriate for this landscape.

I snuck several glances through the giant arch of Angel's Window (a nice name) and followed the trail leading out on top of it. Into this jutting platform of limestone, the elements had eroded a huge hole in the rock. The nearly level Tonto Platform lay before me. To the east was Freya Castle, and to the south, Rama Shrine, Vishnu Temple, and Coronado Butte. The massive flat-topped temple to the south was Wotans Throne. I sniffed juniper berries that smelled like gin, tasted green unripened pine nuts from the piñons, and admired the white blossoms of the cliff rose. I caught sight of the Colorado River, a rare glimpse of the muddy green band, flowing past Unkar Delta and Horesehoe Mesa above it. A few butterflies fluttered about on the wind, bright creatures of the canyon country. In 1941, a Russian exile and amateur lepidopterist named Vladimir Nabokov, hiking on the South Rim's Bright Angel Trail, captured a previously undiscovered species of *Neonympha* butterfly. He went on to write a famous novel, about another nymph, *Lolita*. "Obvious Arizona," Nabokov called the Grand Canyon State. *Lolita*'s narrator, Humbert Humbert, observed while visiting the American Southwest that while the clipped and hedged outdoors of Europe might be an appropriate venue for outdoor lovemaking, America's wildlands were downright *uncomfortable*. There is a saying out here that everything in the West stings, sticks, or stinks.

The Grand Canyon is not the deepest canyon in North America. It only appears that way to us when we look at it. Depending on how you measure them, either Hells Canyon in Idaho or Kings Canyon in California is the deepest. Even parts of Desolation Canyon upriver, on the Colorado's tributary, the Green River, over in Utah, are deeper than the Grand Canyon in certain spots. Topographic maps favor Kings as the champ, by measuring the highest peak against the lowest depth at the bottom of the canyon. But the Grand Canyon of the Colorado is the most extreme case of vertical walls rising steeply out of an inner gorge and lining both sides of a river uniformly for hundreds of miles. It appears to the naked eye to be the deepest canyon because of its greater vertical disport. And only a fool would deny the evidence of his own senses. I stared into the canyon and thought, I am nothing.

I MET A German tourist at Walhalla Overlook. There were a lot of Germans in the park, it seemed. Lots of Japanese, too. Oddly enough, among all the homegrown American tourists, there wasn't so much as a single black citizen of the republic present. I had seen only one black person at the Grand Canyon so far—and he spoke with a distinct Caribbean accent, marking him a foreigner.

The German tourist at Walhalla Overlook caught me looking over his rig, a giant Winnebago RV with Wyoming license plates. Next to his land schooner, my Blazer looked like a VW Beetle.

"We didn't always travel in luxury," the man said somewhat defensively when he saw me staring at his rig. "We used to tent out, my wife and I. This is our first time on the North Rim. It's really quite beautiful." His English was splendid; I heard only a hint of an accent. Americans are the only people in the industrialized world who are monolingual, and proud of it.

"You certainly picked the best side of the Grand Canyon to visit," I told him. He introduced himself as a retired high school teacher. He said that he and his wife had been visiting our national parks every year for the past thirty years.

"We have nothing like this in Europe," he said. "Only the Alps," he added as an afterthought. Foreign tourists had good reason to come here; there wasn't too much raw nature left to see in Europe. "You have something very special in your country," he told me.

"Yes, we love our national parks. You have to visit Congress before you can find anyone in America who hates them."

"My wife and I are going to Arches, and we are going to see Capitol Reef for the first time, too," he told me, again in flawless English. I had taken four years of high school French and two semesters of college French, and today, I'm proud to say, I can understand the dialogue in French art-house films only with the help of subtitles.

"Have you ever been to Canyonlands and Island in the Sky mesa?" I asked him. He told me he hadn't, and so I described for him my very favorite park in the Southwest. He said he would definitely try to make it out to Canyonlands. Christ, what the hell was I thinking? Canyonlands was my favorite park precisely because it was the park most devoid of tourists. I was always advising everyone to visit Canyonlands. It was as if I couldn't help myself. Yet this German seemed to be a very decent chap. Much nicer than the German I had met earlier on the canyon rim, who asked me to take his picture and then started ordering me around as if he were Erich von Stroheim directing a movie.

Grand Canyon is the most heavily visited national park, and at times it can be simply too much, a Disneyesque eyesore. In summer, hotels and campgrounds are booked for months in advance and the South Rim drive is little more than a series of parking-lot overlooks. Smog from Las Vegas to the west and a Navajo coal-generating plant to the east drifts on the winds and creates hazes over the canyon (although the Navajo have cut down on their emissions, while Las Vegas is doing nothing to control its obscene growth). Sight-seeing tours buzz the canyon in light planes, and helicopters fly in and out of the canyon (although I had only seen one helicopter all day and it was too far away to make any noise—in the distance it looked like a mechanical dragonfly). On the South Rim, on the three most popular canyon trails, hikers have to share the paths with mules—which means manure and urine on the trail.

And yet there are other, unmaintained trails descending into the canyon: Hermit, Grandview, Tanner, New Hance, Thunder River. . . . On those, one can still encounter solitude, adventure, even danger. And the South Rim, open all year, has to be experienced in wintertime, under a blanket of fresh snow, and free of crowds, before it can be truly appreciated.

I stopped by ranger headquarters to inquire about Point Sublime and find out whether I would need a backcountry permit to camp there.

"The road is impassable even to four-wheel-drive vehicles," the ranger told me bluntly. "Too much downed timber. There's no way you can get out there in your car. Do you have a mountain bike?" I didn't. "Too bad," he said. A mountain bike would get me there handily. It is a twenty-three-mile trek from the road outside the park. Not many tourists make it to Point Sublime. The road is just too difficult even when it is in a passable condition. Clarence Dutton, the famous Grand Canyon geologist and explorer who gave the point its name, described the view as "the most sublime and awe inspiring spectacle in the world." The promontory of Point Sublime juts out farther into the canyon than any other overlook. From there, the South Rim lies only seven miles across the gulf. Eastward, behind low cliffs, rises Shiva Temple—"grandest of all the buttes and the most majestic in aspect," according to Dutton. In *The Monkey Wrench Gang,* the outlaw lovers Hayduke and Bonnie camp illegally at Point Sublime on a honeymoon break from their monkey-wrenching chores. But with the road impassable, it looked as if Point Sublime might have to wait for another year.

I took the road back to Cape Royal and stopped at a trailhead under the pines. Shouldering a light day pack, I headed out onto the trail. The ponderosa pines were well spaced, the trees spread out in this forest. The ground looked as if it had been subjected to a controlled burn, blackened in patches, green in others. The air was cool and fragrant with piney breezes and the trail climbed upward. An hour later, I stood on the rim, looking out over Cape Final. And I had it all to myself. Cape Final wasn't Point Sublime, but it was sublime enough.

I listened to birds cheeping in the canyon. Caught sight of a Bell's vireo jumping about in the branches of a tall pine. Stared out at the banded palisades on the far rim: orange-and-red sculptured walls dotted with green junipers; amphitheaters and limestone benches and magnificent overhangs. It was never the same; each passing cloud recast it. A cloud would throw its shadow into the canyon and the scene changed. The buttes seemed to rise up to touch each passing shadow. Alcoves deepened or receded back into the rock face as light and shadow changed on the walls.

Feeling thirsty—I was always thirsty in this dry climate—I took another healthy gulp from my canteen. Water was all around and yet unavailable. In the Colorado River, so far down that its sound among the rocks was lost to us up here on the rim. In the cumulonimbus, which were great container ships of vapor drifting across an incandescent sky and changing the visual tone of the canyon. And in caverns deep within the shales under my feet. All of it well out of reach. Those dying of thirst up on the rims had only to look a mile below for a good refreshing drink— the Colorado, a mere five Empire State Buildings down.

Deep in the redrock canyon were green pockets of life. Seeps trickled unexpectedly out of moss-covered cracks in the naked rock. Springs that leaked from openings in the walls supported hanging gardens of vegetation like Elves Chasm. There was even a river—Thunder River—that shot right out of the naked rock wall. Greenery clung to the Redwall Limestone in wet places in the side canyons, on rock walls hung with ferns, orchids, and red and yellow monkey flowers. Leafy green cottonwoods surrounded Deer Falls, Thunder River, Vasey's

Paradise. . . . And, of course, there was Havasu Canyon, green-
est ravine of them all. It would be nice to see Havasu again, I
thought. It was an out-of-the-way branch of the Grand Canyon,
approachable only from the South Rim or by a rafting trip
down the Colorado River. I had had the great good luck to
explore Havasu on my first visit to the Grand Canyon eleven
years before and I had never forgotten the experience. I had a
strong desire to see Havasu one more time. Perhaps I would
end my trip there. Return home by way of the South Rim, and
see Havasu once again. It was certainly something to consider.

I returned to Bright Angel Point to use the North Rim's tourist facilities. Well, no getting around it. A crowded parking lot.
A post office. A general store. Coin laundry and showers. The
nearby campground where I was staying. Something has to
give when a lot of people want to visit a single place. Fortunately, there is only one hotel up on the North Rim—the Grand
Canyon Lodge, and it is a beaut, no denying it. A stunning rock
and timber structure located very close to Bright Angel Point,
designed by a disciple of Frank Lloyd Wright. Its giant picture
windows look out over Transept Canyon.

The North Rim is the connoisseur's rim of the Grand
Canyon, no question about it. But even up here, there was no
getting away from the museum feel of so much of the Grand
Canyon. I think all of us would agree that the wilder a place
like the Grand Canyon remains, the better. Probably all of us
understand that deep down. But a development has been allowed to take place even on the North Rim, which is like a
form of vandalism. It hurts to see the wild places spoiled, for
it is like vandalism against ourselves.

Genesis got it wrong. The earth isn't a heap of raw materials
given to man by God for his exclusive use and profit. A single
breed of chattering ape cannot lay claim to it all. We are only
a small part of a larger creation, and how soon we forget that.

4

CANYON SHANGRI-LA

THAT NIGHT IN camp, after turning in early, I thought about Havasu Canyon and my first visit to the Southwest. Earlier in the evening, wind and rainsqualls had chased me away from the sunset on Bright Angel Point. Malignant storm clouds darkened the western sky, shortening the purple display of twilight. It was freezing in camp; temperatures were plunging. I curled up in my sleeping bag, trying to make the most of its warmth, and thought about the first time I had seen the desert Southwest.

I am at essence an easterner. I was born in Maine and raised for the most part on the Middle Atlantic seaboard. I grew up near the Pine Barrens and shore towns of southern New Jersey. And I made my living as a newspaper reporter there. One summer, I decided that I would take a short leave of absence from my job and spend a month to six weeks fishing for trout in and around Yellowstone National Park. I had often spent my summer and autumn vacations in Wyoming and Montana. But this time, I decided, I would also set aside a week to take a long drive through the desert Southwest, which I had never visited.

I would see the that area and then drive up to Yellowstone for my trout-fishing vacation.

Now this is going to sound silly. I had planned my desert itinerary largely around Edward Abbey's *The Monkey Wrench Gang*. That novel had a very special place on my shelf. In fact, I had long admired all of Abbey's writing, but, rather illogically, I hadn't yet gotten around to seeing the Southwest. It was my intention on this trip to make up for that fact and visit most of the scenes in *The Monkey Wrench Gang* as a kind of half-assed homage to the book. I wanted to see the land that had enlivened the drama.

It took me three days of hard driving to get from New Jersey to Grand Junction, Colorado. Descending from the western slope of the Rocky Mountains the next day, I was treated to a hawk's-eye view of the redrock deserts of Utah. I couldn't believe what I saw—an intricately carved canyon land of hoodoos, slickrock, and mesas under an electric blue sky. Snowy points on the La Sal Mountains, deserts and canyon below. I felt like a hawk gazing down at plateaus of naked pink rock.

I explored Moab and Arches and hiked in Canyonlands. Camped at Natural Bridges in the high piñon forest. Followed the jumbled canyons down into Arizona, drove past Black Mesa, where the Monkey Wrench Gang derailed the coal train, and arrived at Page, where I spent an uncomfortable night. Saw the horrible dam that doomed Glen Canyon under its hateful blue reservoir. Followed the Vermilion Cliffs to Navajo Bridge and Lees Ferry and fished for trout in the copper light of the Colorado River. Continued on the winding road up to Jacob Lake and the North Rim of the Grand Canyon. Hiked the cool forests of the Kaibab Plateau. Walked down to Roaring Springs. Listened to the wind soughing in the pines. Stared over the rim into the abyss.

Someone at the lodge mentioned Havasu Canyon to me.

Suggested I check it out. It was a little out of my way—a great deal out of my way, actually—but it sounded like a capital idea. I remembered well what Edward Abbey had to say about Havasu in *Desert Solitaire*. It got an entire chapter. Abbey was on his way to visit LA by way of the Grand Canyon, had made a side trip to Havasu on a whim, and had lingered there for five weeks. He had the great good luck to see the canyon before tourists found it.

In order to get to Havasu, I drove back down to Lees Ferry, recrossed Navajo Bridge, and skirted the South Rim of the Grand Canyon, with its terrible traffic jams and crowds. I found a dirt road on the Coconino Plateau, which took me into the Hualapai Indian Reservation and on to Hualapai Hilltop at the head of the canyon. Dawn was breaking. It was all on foot from there.

I confess I was a bit apprehensive about going down into Havasu. In addition to all the good things, I had heard some troubling rumors about the place. The tribal teens were heavily into reggae, growing pot, going around stoned, and acting like Rasta men. There had been some trouble at the August peach festival a few years back. A photojournalist for a music magazine had been forcibly detained by a drunken tribal chief after a concert. Her helicopter pilot had to free her and fly her out of the canyon.

Despite this, Havasu is the fairest canyon in the American Southwest. Its creek makes it so. *Havasupai* means "people of the blue-green waters," and Havasu Creek is indeed blue-green like no other stream I have ever seen. Not even the pale blue spring-fed waters of the Little Colorado match it. Its water spouts magically from artesian springs and runs down a red limestone canyon into green cottonwoods and spray-misted ferns, its ravishing waterfalls plunging over terraces into pools of unforgettable turquoise. Havasu Canyon is the home of the

Havasupai, all six hundred or so of them, the last remaining Indian inhabitants of the Grand Canyon. They grow peaches, figs, melons, and sweet corn in a canyon Shangri-la. My plan was to stay in a campground used primarily by hikers and young European budget travelers.

The sun was just beginning to rise over the tan cliffs of the Coconino Plateau. I could see the dark trail below me. Leaving the car at Hualapai Hilltop, I cinched up my backpack and began the eight-mile descent into the canyon. A helicopter service took tourists down into Supai, but that felt wrong to me. I wanted to descend the Hualapai Trail the old-fashioned way, on foot—the way people have been doing it for centuries. I figured it would take about four hours to reach the village.

The trail was dry and dusty and the canyon rim brightening with early morning light. By midday, the temperatures would reach a hundred degrees at the bottom of the canyon. Some time back, the Havasupai had rejected a scheme by the Bureau of Indian Affairs to blast a road into their village that would funnel in mass tourism. Wisely, the Havasupai had decided there would be no road leading in or out of the canyon. A pity they hadn't felt the same way about helicopters.

I heard hooves clopping and animals snorting. Three times, I was backed against the wall of the narrow switchback as horses and riders, and finally a mule team, passed me on their way up the canyon. One teenage wrangler, his long, shiny black hair cinched by a red bandanna, led a pair of empty mounts. Another boy guided horses laden with empty saddlebags. The Havasupai wranglers would pick up tourists, mail, and supplies up on Hualapai Hilltop. Supai was the only community in the United States that had its mail delivered by mule; it said so on the postmark.

After a while, I could smell water and vegetation down in the canyon. The trail followed a draw where a handful of pools had survived the last rain. Ravens flew overhead and lizards scattered at my approach.

Eventually, I saw signs of Supai Village. The canyon widened down there. Planted fields and tractors came into view. The prefab houses of the Havasupai looked very small under towering walls of red limestone. A few TV satellite dishes were visible. Laundry flapped on clotheslines. A little girl was brushing down a horse.

I looked for the Havasupai Tourist Enterprise Office. All visitors were required to check in there. A few Indians were lounging by the post office, smoking cigarettes and speaking to one another in Havasupai, a Yuman dialect heard only in this canyon. It is distinct from the Uto-Aztecan tongue of the Hopi and the Athabascan speech of the Navajo. The men noticed me listening and fell silent, so I walked on. Many Indians went about their routines as if there weren't *haigu* in their midst; they had perfected the art of making us invisible.

I spotted hikers resting on benches outside a ranch house that I took to be the tourist office. I got in line to buy my permit and pay a camping fee. A soft-spoken official, whose last name was Uqualla, was patiently explaining to some French-Canadian hikers that they couldn't stay if they didn't have reservations. They were going to have a long hike back out of the canyon. The campground fills up quickly in Havasu, and reservations are required weeks in advance. Sometimes the office phone goes unanswered for hours and even days.

"How's the trout fishing?" I asked Mr. Uqualla.

"No *aigee* up here. You have to go all the way down to Beaver Falls to catch trout." He quickly gave me directions to Beaver Falls, naming the other waterfalls that I would have to pass in order to get there. Beaver Falls was a four-mile hike from the village of Supai, he told me, and well past the campground. I wanted to ask him what happened to the trout above the falls, but Mr. Uqualla had a line of impatient hikers to check in.

Back outside, I looked over a visitor's lodge constructed in the style of a modern motel. Its rooms would set a tourist back a pretty penny. I guess if you could afford the helicopter ride down to the reservation, you could afford a room in this lodge. The Havasupai might be the most isolated of any Indian tribe in Arizona, but they were doing fairly well, relatively speaking. Twenty thousand tourists passed through their canyon every year.

Well, they had their modest prosperity coming. The Havasupai had made a home here for centuries. In winter, the tribe hunted deer up on the Coconino Plateau; in summer they farmed the floor of Havasu Canyon. But as whites began moving into the Grand Canyon, the Indians found themselves increasingly restricted. President Teddy Roosevelt asked them to clear out to make way for a new national park, but they protested. By midcentury, they found themselves confined within one square mile of the canyon. It wasn't until the 1970s, through lawsuits and political action, that they won back much of their ancestral land from the federal government.

Lugging my backpack, I headed down the dusty canyon trail toward the campground. I found it a mile and a half farther down the trail, well away from the central village. By now, I had noticed mosquitoes and other insects humming in the air and I began to smell riverine vegetation. Havasu Creek was down there in the fresh willows and cottonwoods, breathing life into the desert canyon.

I came upon Navajo Falls, the first of three major cascades. It dropped eighty-three feet into a lush ravine filled with ferns misted by spray. The creek wound through twisting grapevines and leafy cottonwood shade that diffused the bright desert light. The water had formed beautiful travertine dams, semi-circular ridges of whitish rock, that pooled the waters.

A few hundred yards downstream, Havasu Falls plunged one hundred feet into a pool as blue as the Virgin's cloak. The creek was the color of the sky, reflected by a whitened streambed and by white mineral particles in the water. The mineral particles came from dissolving calcium carbonate found in the Redwall Limestone, the canyon rock that was being cut by the downward progress of the stream. These limestone deposits had built up over the creek bed, hardening into travertine. Where logjams and debris had once blocked the creek, the travertine had formed into stony barriers much like little dams. These travertine blockages had transformed the entire creek into a seemingly unending staircase of falls, cascades, and pools.

Viewed from above, the pools under the waterfalls were as blue as morning glories. The water was white where it plunged and foamed, spreading into a Caribbean blue in a widening circle around the plunge point, and finally greening in the shallows. Havasu Falls sprayed a theatrical mist onto the Redwall Limestone, leaving behind a hardened tapestry of travertine.

Green cottonwoods brought relief to the hot canyon. An olive light filtered down through tunnels of willow, hackberry, grapevine, box elder, and flickering velvet ash. Lush moss and maidenhair ferns grew around the splashing pools. The creek gave life to scarlet monkey flowers, blue-and-purple monks-hood, stalks of lupine, and the red spikes of cardinal flowers. I saw goldfinches and red summer tanagers flashing in the canyon.

I followed Havasu Creek for another mile down its redwall canyon, until a walk through the campground brought me to the top of the most spectacular falls of all. Mooney Falls dropped two hundred feet into a pool of turquoise magic. The Havasupai had named it after "Crazy Mooney," a miner who fell to his death here. Dan Mooney's ghost, the Havasupai say, is still digging away in the cave below the falls. The pool acted as a giant reflector, mirroring the Redwall Limestone and green foliage of the canyon and absorbing it into the faultless blue of the Arizona sky.

A very steep trail led down to the pool, which was full of swimmers. People were shouting and jumping from over-hanging boulders, and I heard several foreign languages being spoken. I dove into the pool and swam as close as I could get to the thundering mist below the falls. I felt energized by the negative ions. Sinking into the lime water, I surrendered all care to Havasu Creek. Drifting toward the raised lip of the pool, I braced my feet against the rimstone dam, gazing upward at the curving red terraces of limestone draped in tangles of wild grapevine and maidenhair fern. The pool was pure refresh-ment.

I spent the remainder of the afternoon there. Time passed too quickly, and yet it did not seem to pass at all. Finally, with the sun's glare well off the pools, and shadows dimming the canyon, I returned to the campground, where earlier I had stashed my rucksack. The campground was located be-tween Mooney and Havasu falls, and in the early-evening light, tents had sprung up everywhere. I lined up for fresh water where a spring flowed out of a fern-covered wall. I was drinking a gallon a day in the desert heat. The canyon was cooling down now. The aroma of dinners cooking on propane camp stoves rose and drifted on the air. No campfires, though—a rule against open fires was strictly enforced. Some backpackers were strumming guitars and singing around the lights of lanterns. A few poker games got going and no doubt more than one bottle was making its rounds. I turned in early, exhausted from the day's hike. I must have covered fourteen miles. I unrolled my sleeping bag under the brilliant desert stars and fell asleep with the sound of the creek running in the rocks and in my head.

BIRDSONG FILLED THE pastel dawn. The sky was a nacreous shell of pale blues and pinks, peach and gold. I headed out of the campground early, bound for Beaver Falls. I wanted to get in some fishing before rafting parties down on the Colorado River started hiking up into Havasu Canyon. Twenty-one commercial river outfitters offered Grand Canyon water tours. What was once a white-water wilderness experience on the mighty Colorado had now become routine fun. And every outfitter stopped at the mouth of Havasu Canyon.

I hiked down the canyon, and mile after mile, the pools continued through a landscape of rouge-colored cliffs, riverine groves, and uninterrupted beauty. Each bend brought me to yet another waterfall spilling over a travertine dam. Moss grew like bright coral on the creek bed. I'd cool off and let the waterfalls douse me. I imagined it would be much like this all the way down to the floor of the Grand Canyon.

At last, I came upon Beaver Falls, a rocky staircase of many falls, dropping twenty or so feet straight down into scalloped, fluted basins. The travertine dams were a whitish tan and were uniformly smooth from bank to bank. I could see the fossilized impressions of logjams in the calcified limestone.

I fished below Beaver Falls, working the water with my fly rod. The canyon walls narrowed the farther downstream I went. I was starting to see the crimson-tipped blossoms of cacti, yucca, and spiny ocotillos, a sure sign I was in the lower Sonoran life zone. Where the cliffs narrowed, the stream reflections and albedo waves flickered on the Redwall Limestone.

I searched the stream with my fly rod, making short casts into the calmer pockets of water. Without much difficulty, I caught a squirming eight-inch rainbow trout. Rainbow trout swim up Havasu Creek from the Colorado River. Once, the Colorado had been a golden silt-laden catfish stream. A warm reddish brown Colorado. But Glen Canyon Dam at Lake Powell changed it. Now the Grand Canyon's water is cold and aquamarine, supports lots of trout, and is controlled by the upstream discharge of turbines. As much as I love trout fishing, I'm sure I would have preferred the old, red Colorado.

A young Havasupai boy was walking up the path with a stringer of dead trout hanging from his belt. He stopped and we talked. He told me that the trout fishing was good all the way from Beaver Falls downstream. He asked me why I let my trout go, and I explained to him my catch-and-release philosophy. I asked him if he was a Bob Marley fan. He said yes, but he was more into heavy metal now. He waved good-bye and disappeared up the trail, no doubt laughing at the *haigu* who let all his trout go.

Havasu Canyon was filling up now. People were splashing in the stream, their voices ringing all over the canyon. Trout fishing would be futile now. The first of what would be many rafting parties had arrived. I overheard one of the naturalist river guides speaking to his group about uranium mining up on the Coconino Plateau, just outside the park boundary. I was vaguely familiar with the controversy. A mining conglomerate had sunk a shaft into Red Butte, a sacred mountain of the Havasupai. Red Butte is the abdomen of the Spirit Mother, who each year gives birth to a renewal of life, resting her newborn on her belly briefly before sending it out into the world. Environmentalists saw another kind of sacrilege. They warned that a uranium mine on Red Butte threatened the drainage of Cataract Creek, the headwaters of Havasu Canyon. The Havasupai feared, with good reason, that Havasu might become contaminated with radioactive mine tailings.

I spotted a lone man, who appeared to be a Havasupai, walking down the trail toward me. He had that extra roll of fat around his gut that all Havasupai adults seem to develop. This has been attributed to a so-called thrifty gene that many desert Indians have. A thrifty metabolism allows them to store up energy on the meager pickings of the desert but has left them prone to obesity now that they have switched to a modern American diet heavy in fat and sugar. The man was delighted to see me with a fly rod and wanted to know how I had done.

Sam Archuleta was his name. He told me he hand-lined trout, spinning the baited monofilament like a lasso when making his casts. He liked to fish down on the Colorado where the trout were larger, and hunt deer up on the plateau. I asked Sam why there were few, if any, trout above Beaver Falls. There was speculation that raw sewage, dumped into the creek before a septic system was installed, might have been at fault. But Sam said the creek was just fished out. "We ate them all," he explained with a laugh.

Sam told me he had teenage sons who were caught up in the reggae craze that had swept the reservation. Sam thought the problem with the Havasupai youth was that they were bored. There was nothing to do in paradise. Many of the young regarded reggae as a religion and marijuana as a sacrament, and this upset him. While Sam wasn't exactly a traditionalist, he feared a spiritual breach within his tribe. I asked him about the uranium mine on Red Butte. "Reggae's just a fad," he said. "But radiation, well, there's no getting rid of that." We parted, Sam wishing me good fishing.

I walked the centuries-old rock path made slippery by the spraying mist from Havasu Falls. I found a boulder close by the continuous turbulence of the racing creek as it soared over the edge, and from this throne, I contemplated the falls, the travertine, the red tanagers darting around the chasm, and the seeming isolation. It all struck me as utterly wild and eternal.

But the wonder of the Grand Canyon is that it is not everlasting. We only see the landscape as timeless. In reality, life is fleeting down here in Havasu Canyon. The oasis is a fragile world. Havasu Creek doesn't flow into eternity; rather, it flows into our times.

5

A GRAND STAIRCASE

I AWOKE TO gray skies and snow flurries. The wind had blown in the yellow pines all night long and the sound was like a constant waterfall. The temperature was thirty-five degrees, but it was snowing lightly. The flurries blew about in the wind. I broke camp. I'd only reserved two nights on the North Rim campground. I had planned to rough it and camp at Point Sublime, hiking out there on foot on the timber-downed trail, then decided against it because of the weather. I could pitch a tent outside the park, in the national forest, where there was free dispersed camping. Or I could move on to Utah, where it would be warmer. I thought about hiking down the Kaibab Trail to Roaring Springs, but I had done that on an earlier trip; and I didn't like the way the weather was turning up here on the North Rim.

It would be interesting to see Havasu Canyon again. Three years after my trip to Havasu, a particularly ferocious flash flood scoured the canyon, forcing villagers to flee temporarily to higher ground and wiping out 70 percent of the ancient cottonwood trees. It would be interesting to see the place once again. See how its green cottonwoods had grown back. See if it was still the fairest canyon in the Southwest. Perhaps I would end my trip down there, at the South Rim. After circumventing the Colorado Plateau and visiting the highlands of northern New Mexico, I could return home by way of the South Rim of the Grand Canyon and visit Havasu one more time. At least that was my plan. Close the circle.

I took the road out of the park and back into the national forest. As the elevation dropped, the temperatures rose slightly. I dropped down out of the forested plateau and had good views of the Vermilion Cliffs. Broad slant beams of lemon light shot through the gray clouds, falling on isolated spots on the Vermilion Cliffs. The cliffs glowed deep red on those panels where a stormy sunlight illuminated them. I would be driving directly through an opening in those cliffs into Utah. The legendary Grand Staircase began just below those ridges.

When the Colorado Plateau uplifted millions of years ago, it left behind a series of south-facing cliffs on what is now the Arizona-Utah border. These cliff-wall terraces, each a different age, and each named for its distinct coloring, climb north from the Grand Canyon to even higher plateaus in Utah. The land rises thousands of feet at a time, up five steps, the Grand Staircase.

First in line are the Chocolate Cliffs, which begin in Arizona. Rising above them are the flushed red colors of the Vermilion Cliffs. Above the Vermilion Cliffs is an escarpment of Navajo sandstone known as the White Cliffs, tan in color, but glowing almost sugar white in the brilliant Utah sunshine. In Zion National Park, where I was headed, the Virgin River cuts through both the Vermilion and White cliffs, creating an unforgettable canyon. Above the White Cliffs are the Gray Cliffs, less perpendicular and less interesting to look at. The famous Pink Cliffs come at the final step in the Grand Staircase. This is the fantastic siltstone and limestone out of which Bryce Canyon was cut. Because of the great distance between the steps, the staircase is not visible to the naked eye at ground level.

I drove to Kanab, Utah. The sky had cleared, the sun was shining on the Vermilion Cliffs, and the air was very warm— the way you would expect it to be in the desert in summertime. At Mount Carmel Junction, I came upon the eastern entrance to Zion National Park. Here was a dramatic and bizarre landscape, even by Utah standards. Giant sloping sandstone mesas and hills had weathered white and the piñon and junipers seemed to grow out of solid rock. I found myself in a slickrock landscape of beehives, stone mushrooms, king-size footstools, and miniature capped pillars. But the most notable erosion on this high plateau could be seen in the fantastic checkerboarding on many of the hillsides. Looming before everything was the great mound of sandstone known as the Checkerboard Mesa. The face of Checkerboard Mesa had creased into a million squares, a classic example of a geologic process known as crossbedding, in which the cracks in the rock develop horizontally as well as vertically. The horizontal lines follow the beds of ancient sand dunes. The vertical cracks were caused by straining along set joints, either when the land uplifted in ancient times or expanded and contracted from the heat and cold.

I passed through two tunnels under the sandstone cliffs, the first only five hundred feet long, the second more than a mile in length. Even with my car lights on, the tunnel was a claustrophobic nightmare, only twenty-two feet wide and sixteen feet high. There was a long wait for tour buses and RVs to be escorted through the two-way traffic.

I came out into a different world. Great monoliths of dark red rock rose up into brilliant white sandstones. Here were outstanding views of East and West Temple and the Sentinel. I caught sight of Zion's Great Arch. I descended into the canyon down a series of hairpin switchbacks and a tire blew out on my Blazer on the narrow washboard road. By the time I got to the bottom, the tire was in shreds.

I stopped to change the flat but couldn't locate the Blazer's spare. A park ranger who was driving by stopped and helped me find the spare under the car (it was well hidden) and then, well beyond the call of duty, he offered to change it for me. Imagine your average highway patrolman doing that! It made me think of how park rangers and lifeguards (think of *Baywatch*) are the only law-enforcement officers who are both universally beloved and instinctively trusted by citizens. Rangers are the luckiest of law officers, not only because of the marvelous work they do and the splendid environs in which they get to do it but also because the citizens regard them with such deep and abiding affection. I mean, nobody ever feels that way about cops. Most of us don't even think of rangers as being cops, having badges and guns and power of arrest. And of course they aren't cops; they're *rangers*.

There was a huge hole in the sidewall; the tire was shot, so I wasted a couple hours in Springdale, the town just outside the park's western entrance, as repairmen awaited delivery of a new tire. The Firestone center in Springdale was a gold mine. The owner told me tourists were forever suffering blowouts inside the park. I killed time by strolling about the streets of the small town, gazing up at the redrock of the Vermilion Cliffs and admiring the orange Engelmann prickly pear and purple torch cacti in bloom. A line of low, dark clouds was edging out the sun in the west. Finally, the tire was replaced, and I drove back into Zion National Park just as a series of brief thunderstorms hit.

The afternoon was punctuated by thunder and brilliant sun showers. I headed up Zion Canyon Scenic Drive. Green translucent cottonwoods lined the banks of the Virgin River. Zion was a wilderness gallery of hanging stone. Massive half domes and temples rimmed the great canyon on both sides of the highway. Immense rock murals, stained with streaks of orangish red color and black desert varnish, dropped a sheer fifteen hundred feet below white-domed uplands. Flowing water had carved the rock into slot canyons, deep alcoves, and massive walls. The Navajo sandstone created a polished beauty where it outcropped, flowing into lines of grace and power.

Zion's massive hanging rocks, erosion-carved sandstone formations, megaliths of nature with names like the Great White Throne, Court of the Patriarchs, and Mountain of the Sun, towered above the river. Waterfalls freshened by rain cascaded over the rims of the great formations. A neck-craning two-thousand-foot cliff of Navajo sandstone known as the Streaked Wall rose at the head of the Scenic Drive, its cliff face painted with the stains of organic material that had leached out from the pine forest atop the cliff. On the roof of the Streaked Wall were the easily recognizable Beehives, formed when cement in the sandstone washed out of the rock. Where the road curved to the left, the so-named Twin Brothers rose up, appearing at first as separate rocks, but actually joined together by a U-shaped saddle—Siamese twins, if you will. Just north of these buttes stood Mountain of the Sun, so called because the dawn light struck it first. I noticed a honeycomb appearance in the sandstone peaks across the river. Water seeping down joints and cracks in the rock had percolated out, eliminating cementing sandstones, leaving a honeycomb wall behind. Beyond was the Court of the Patriarchs and their three peaks, Abraham, Isaac, and Jacob. In the land of Mormon, many of the prominent landmarks in Zion Canyon had actually been named by a Methodist ecclesiastic from Ogden, Frederick Vining Fisher.

At their base, these monoliths were redrock. As they rose

upward, the dark stone began to lighten into a shining gold and white. Most of the red-producing iron oxide had leached out, leaving behind blond cliffs above. Cementing stones had weakened, leaving these rocks softer and rounder.

I found the Virgin River high and discolored. The Firestone manager in Springdale who had changed my flat tire had told me that the Virgin had been running high all spring because of El Niño. He said that despite its trouty appearance, there were no trout to be found in the warm desert river. Its banks were thick with tall cottonwoods, box elders, and velvet ash. I noticed a black-chinned hummingbird and a pair of warbling vireos.

Dodging raindrops, I walked the footpath to Weeping Rock. The moist nooks in the alcove were overflowing with a lush mossy growth, scarlet and yellow monkey flowers, and wet maidenhair fern clinging to bare rock and even dangling upside down from overhangs. The rock was weeping rainwater. Not this day's rain, but a rainwater collected in the porous sandstone above the alcove. Rainwater that had fallen onto the plateau high above Weeping Rock about two years earlier. The rainwater had slowly percolated down two thousand feet through porous grains of sandstone until reaching a harder layer of clay, and now it was seeping out at the canyon's spring line.

From the alcove of this dripping spring, I had a splendid view of Angels Landing, so named because it looks as if only an angel could land atop it. And behind it was the Great White Throne, the most famous monolith in Zion Park. "I have looked for this mountain all my life," wrote the Methodist minister Frederick Vining Fisher, "but I never expected to find it in this world. It is the Great White Throne."

The road followed the canyon for a mile, and the towering cliffs seemed to press in closer. Shadows deepened, and vegetation grew more abundant and lush. I came to the end of the road, a circular parking lot, deep within what is known as the Temple of Sinawava, named in honor of the wolf god of the Paiute Indians. Across the river was a towering rostrum of sandstone known as the Pulpit. From here, a footpath followed the river for a mile toward what is called the Gateway to the Narrows.

I had intended to follow the canyon up past the Narrows. Here the walls closed in to the width of the riverbed. The sky narrowed to a slot above the canyon. I had to wade directly in the river to explore further—the canyon was just that narrow. Here were cliffs two thousand feet high, and in places a pair of hikers with outstretched arms could reach across the river from wall to wall. But the Virgin was running too high to make wading possible. And there was too great a danger of drowning in a flash flood. Under optimum conditions, a hearty hiker could continue up the canyon for sixteen miles, scrambling over rocks and wading chest-high, the clear water winding through the canyon in a golden glow of refracted sunlight. Reluctantly, I turned around.

As I drove back through rain and sun showers, the views looked somehow different. I was seeing the galleries at different angles. Also, the light seemed to be forever changing. I drove slowly, enjoying the rainsqualls and sunbursts.

I had managed to secure a tent site at Watchman Campground earlier, and just within minutes of its filling up. The campground was set in an old fruit and pecan orchard near the western entrance to the park. Campgrounds fill up quickly in Zion. The park is only 158 miles from teeming Las Vegas. It was not yet summer, schools were still in session, and yet Zion's two campgrounds were full. In Zion, footpaths like the Riverside Walk, and the trail leading up to Weeping Rock, had to be paved over, a necessary evil to prevent the hordes from trampling everything to death.

The campground was named after Watchman, a 2,600-foot mountain guarding the eastern entrance. Strictly speaking, it's not accurate to call these peaks mountains. Zion's temples and buttes are actually the carved edges of the canyon's Kolob Terrace. Mountain or not, Watchman glowed with an unworldly grandeur in the fading light of sundown. And because inspecting sunsets is in my line, I spent a lot of time watching it.

The ground was rock-hard. I couldn't get the stakes pounded to set up my tent. My campsite neighbor, an amateur rock hound, saw me struggling and loaned me his geologist's hammer and spike. Friendly westerners were always doing me favors. The man told me he was a retired oilman and lived in Sun City, just outside of Las Vegas; he traveled in one of those small flatbed campers that fold out. Very handy. I admired RVs, even though I was always getting stuck behind them on the highway. They are the devil's own vehicles, but funny how they are always driven by the nicest people you'll ever meet. My neighbor spoke with a foreign accent and told me he was of Polish descent. He said he loved living in Sun City; It was convenient to places like Zion.

Zion, beautiful and stunning though it was, seemed a little too controlled and manicured for my taste. Too many compromises, such as paved footpaths, neutralizing the wilderness. It was a case of plenty of beauty and not enough wildness. Too much traffic, too many parking lots. Just too many people. I don't know what the answer for that is. Probably more parks. Try telling that to the nature haters in Congress.

The rainstorm had passed over Zion. Watchman stood golden against a wine-dark sky. Zion's temple rims were radiant with alpen glow. As I prepared the evening meal, a yellow half-moon rose out of the east and put another face on Watchman. I sat for a long time digesting my supper and contemplating the moonlit rock looming above my camp. I felt none of the canyon's foreboding. The Paiute would not linger in Zion Canyon after dark. Perhaps the enormity of the place weighed down their spirits. I rolled up in the sleeping bag and for a long while listened to the night before joining it.

I awoke in the middle of the night, badly in need of a pee. It was freezing outside. The moon was down, the night ablaze with cold stars. I could actually see the hazy band of the Milky Way. I thought, This is the way it should always be.

IF ZION IS MASSIVE, Bryce Canyon is delicate.

Bryce is not really a canyon, but the intricately eroded edge of a plateau. After a brief drive north from Zion up the final step in the Grand Staircase the following morning, I came out onto a high evergreen plateau. Emerging on foot from the pines at the cliff edge, I gazed down into an amphitheater filled with thousands of rock hoodoos resembling beautifully carved chess pieces.

A tide of morning light flooded a wonderland of banded rock spires. This fairyland was more brilliant in color and tone than even the Grand Canyon. I stared down at the fantastically carved and cored rock. The Paiute believed these pillars were evil men turned into stone by the Great Spirit and condemned to stand mute forever. Served them right.

I faced this vast expanse of multicolored spires and saw ruined castles, crenelated battlements, and delicate minarets. Pillars by the thousands stood like toy soldiers. Below me were numerous alcoves, grottos, narrow defiles and box canyons. The rocks were pink as hams, salmon-colored, orange, yellow, and umber. Iron oxide brought out the red tones in the rock. Where there were hints of purple and magenta, manganese was at work. The changing colors made the canyon look fleeting. Here was a wedding-cake frosting of badlands more delicate and intricate than any erosion I had ever seen. Water was the sculptor—water in the form of snow, rain, and ice eating away the plateau. And coldness, the cold cracking and splitting sandstone and limestone. Bryce is nine thousand feet above sea level, and temperatures drop to freezing an average of two hundred nights a year.

The view of this festive bazaar continued across a plateau broken by cliffs and the canyon of the Paria River. Beyond were snow-tipped mountains, evergreen forests, and meadows. And there was Navajo Mountain, a spirit cone floating in the far distance.

A feature of Bryce Canyon is that the colors change with each passing hour. At sunrise, the amphitheater glows with deep reds and furnace oranges, the hoodoos reflecting back the golden sunlight of early morning. As the day lengthens, the reds fade and pinks and whites of multiple hue appear, until the noon sun fades out much of the color. By late afternoon, the hoodoos again are orange, and at sundown the pinks return. As shadows reach out from the rim, rock spires redden and deepen to purple and finally blacken into darkness.

Looking down at the orange labyrinth was as mesmerizing as staring into a fire. The wonderfully eroded pillars had created a fairy-tale world. At Sunrise Point, I headed down the trail that leads to the Queens Garden. The trailside was bright with pink and yellow cactus blooms. The footpath wound around the rock formation known as Gulliver's Castle, took turns through several short tunnel arches, and ended at a small grove of piñon. At the bottom of this rock garden, standing high on a pedestal, was the stately figure of Queen Victoria herself. She looked oddly regal for someone stuck in cowboy country.

Back up on the rim, at Inspiration Point, I viewed Silent City, a mysterious and deserted abode of thin spires with melting candle shapes. Water erosion had created freestanding walls of fantastic organ pipe. The rock formations in Bryce seemed to be lined up in splendidly carved rows, especially close by the plateau's rim, where the elements had not yet whittled down the artwork to isolated spires and pedestals.

I took in sundown from Bryce Point. Here was my best view yet of the amphitheater. To the west, under the plateau, stood a rock palisade called the Wall of Windows. Harder limestones above had resisted erosion, while the softer siltstones beneath had washed out, leaving a wall of windows and Gothic arches worthy of a medieval cathedral. I looked down upon hikers straggling out of the amphitheater along the Peekaboo Loop. They were small enough to appear toylike, yet their voices carried clearly up to me on the point.

Violet-green swallows and white-throated swifts whirled and dive-bombed in the final light. Evening shadows crept up the formations, which were turning pink, then red, then lavender. The temperature dropped with alarming abruptness.

Gazing down into the maze of pagodas and box canyons, I thought of Ebenezer Bryce, an early Mormon settler who first ranched this country. A man more concerned with wrestling a living out of the land than rhapsodizing over it, he had this to say about the canyon named in his honor: "Helluva place to lose a cow."

Set well off from the rim of the badlands amphitheater, and mostly hidden behind a screen of pines, was the parking lot and visitor's center. The Park Service had done a very good job concealing the human clutter. But there was no escaping this man-made world. No matter from what viewpoint you stood up there on the rim, you could always catch a glimpse of the lot behind the trees. And the illusion of wildness was shattered. I don't know what the cure for this is.

6

SUNDOWN LEGEND

I DROVE INTO Escalante, a tiny town on the edge of the Kai-
parowits Plateau, population 818, including household pets. I
stopped at a sporting-goods store to replenish my supply of
tent stakes, and I was pleased and surprised to find a favorite
book on display. I hadn't been able to locate this particular
volume in San Francisco, which has a world-class book market.
I couln't find it in the stacks in the public library, either; I had
to borrow a copy through interlibrary loan. But W. L. Rusho's
Everett Ruess: A Vagabond for Beauty was a best-seller in Escalante, Utah.

There might still be people living in Escalante who remember the day, more than half a century ago, when Everett Ruess
rode into town on his burro. These townsfolk would have been
young children or teenagers back then. But Everett Ruess was
someone not easily forgotten.

I think I am safe in saying that there has never been another
American teenager like Everett Ruess. Everett loved art and
nature, to the exclusion of almost anything else. He followed
his muse into the desert, seeking artistic bliss and oneness with

nature. It must have made for an unusual sight, this teenager
with his burro, rucksack, and painter's kit.

Everett came down with wanderlust at an early age. At sixteen, he set off alone to explore the Sierra Nevada, the California coast, and the desert Southwest. Nothing seemed to daunt
this precocious lad. He exchanged prints with Ansel Adams
and made friends with Edward Weston, Maynard Dixon, and
Dorothea Lange. He was naïve, immature, a dreamer. But there
was a magnificence, too, in the life he chose for himself and in
the things he accomplished in his brief time.

His desire to be an artist was unappeasable. So, too, was his
urgency to explore and enjoy wilderness. He traveled beyond
the safe and familiar, refusing to live an ordinary life. He was a
boy so sensitive to art and nature that he sometimes found
beauty overwhelming and even painful. He recorded his ram-
blings and adventures in his journals and in many revealing letters to friends and family. This early work is what he left behind
as his legacy. For at the age of twenty, Everett disappeared into
the remote canyon country outside of Escalante, never to be seen
again. His life, and the mystery behind his disappearance, is one
of the great sundown legends of the Southwest.

At the time of his disappearance, Everett was already a seasoned wanderer.* The younger of two sons, he began his vag-
abonding while still in high school, encouraged by his mother
in his romantic dreams and wanderlust. Stella Knight Ruess,
who fancied herself an artist, was the principal force behind her
son's nonconformist upbringing, and she raised her boy to be
an artist. Both she and her husband, Christopher, gave their
blessing when their teenage son announced that he wanted to

---

*What follows is based on the account in W. L. Rusho, *Everett Ruess: A Vagabond for
Beauty* (Layton, Utah: Peregrine Smith, 1983).

leave his comfortable middle-class home in Los Angeles to go wandering in the American wilderness.

Everett had his first solo adventure in the summer of 1930, at sixteen, hitchhiking to Big Sur and Carmel to camp on the beaches. He showed up unannounced at the studio of the renowned photographer Edward Weston, and within days he was living there and palling around with the photographer's young sons. Everett had an ability to make friends easily, and he was never shy in the presence of great artists. Everett drew inspiration from the way Weston had organized his life around art and nature.

After a month of painting, sketching, and beachcombing, Everett set out for Yosemite, where he would spend the remainder of his summer holiday. "The valley hardly seemed real at first," Everett wrote his family. He made a long trek into the Yosemite high country, and he thought about getting a burro for his next expedition. Summer ended too soon for him, and Everett was reluctant to return to what he called "the city and its sordid buildings and business places." But he came home to finish his secondary education, graduating from Hollywood High that winter.

A month later, still only sixteen, Everett struck out on his own for Monument Valley, Arizona, a place still relatively unknown in those days. These were the Depression years, and Everett was taking a risk. He arrived in Navajoland in late winter with little money but in high spirits. With the help of an occasional care package from home, he was able to meet his modest needs. He talked a Navajo into selling him a sweet-tempered burro, bargaining him down from twelve to six dollars. He hiked into canyons, forded rivers, made friends with the Navajo, and even built his own log hogans to keep warm. He went to Kayenta and introduced himself to John Wetherill, the famous Indian trader, one of the discoverers of the fabled

Anasazi ruins at Mesa Verde. He picked Wetherill's brains, asking all manner of questions about the desert and the Indians. He explored the local Indian ruins at Keet Seel and Betatakin. Friendships grew out of chance encounters with people he met along the trail. Tad Nichols and Randolph "Pat" Jenks, two Arizona teenagers who gave him a ride through Flagstaff in their pickup, put him up in a homestead cabin and supplied him with groceries. A twenty-five-dollar check, mailed from home, first prize in a poster competition, pleased Everett greatly and was much needed. Everett adopted a month-old Navajo puppy and named him Curly. Curly sometimes rode with him in the saddle. He signed his letters Lan Rameau, his new pen name, and he briefly named his burro Everett.

"The world has seemed to me more beautiful than ever before," Everett wrote to his high school friend Bill Jacobs. "I have loved the red rocks, the twisted trees, the red sand blowing in the wind, the slow, sunny clouds tossing the sky, the shafts of moonlight on my bed at night. I have seemed to be at one with the world."

Everett spent most of August and September at the Grand Canyon, climbing to the bottom and exploring both rims. At first, the ranger wasn't certain whether he should let the kid enter the park on a burro. Initially, Everett's animal balked at crossing the suspension footbridge at the bottom of the canyon. Tourists were constantly asking Everett to pose with his mount.

Everett struck out for Zion Canyon and landed in the hospital for eight days with a royal case of poison ivy. He helped tear down the house of a Mormon bishop, one of the farmers ordered to move because of the expansion of the national park. Writing to his older brother, Waldo, in early October, Everett was able to report that he had crossed the Grand Canyon on the rough Tonto Trail, the only park visitor to do it that year.

"Time and again the burro went off the trail, twice at dangerous places," Everett told Waldo. At Hermit Camp, he saw workers preparing a shooting site for a Fox production of Zane Grey's *The Rainbow Trail.* With cold weather coming on, Everett headed south into the Sonoran Desert. His tramped along the Apache Trail and explored the Tonto cliff dwellings. Both money and grub were running out. "I have been meeting all types of people," Everett wrote Bill Jacobs, "artists, writers, hobos, cooks, cowmen, miners, bootleggers. . . . The bootlegger said that as soon as he sold his stock on hand he could offer me a job guarding his still in the mountains and packing barrels to the retreats."

Everett hitched back home to Los Angeles for Christmas. He had been away eleven months. He resided at home the remainder of that winter, taking off again for Arizona in the spring. He crossed the Painted Desert on horse and burro and explored Canyon de Chelly and Canyon del Muerto in Navajoland. From there, he traveled to southwestern Colorado to visit the Anasazi ruins at Mesa Verde. There is a wonderful photograph of Everett taken at Mesa Verde, showing him holding a live buzzard by the wings.

In a letter to his brother, Waldo, Everett wrote, "I have been thinking more and more that I shall always be a lone wanderer of the wilderness. God, how the trail lures me. You cannot comprehend its resistless fascination for me. After all the lone trail is the best. . . . I'll never stop wandering. And when the time comes to die, I'll find the wildest, loneliest, most desolate spot there is."

Everett hitched his way home (by way of the Grand Canyon), getting stuck in the desert in Needles before managing to flag down a ride. That September, at his father's request, Everett enrolled at UCLA, but he did poorly in most subjects except English and geology, and he dropped out after one semester.

He spent his Christmas break camping in Carmel and Point Lobos, and summer found him wandering in the High Sierras. In autumn, he left for San Francisco to study art formally. Everett immersed himself in the bohemian and cultural life of the city, frequenting art exhibits and attending the symphony and opera. He attached himself to the well-known painter Maynard Dixon and his wife, the photographer Dorothea Lange. "Ansel Adams waxed very enthusiastic about my black and white work," Everett wrote his family. Adams declined to exhibit Everett's work in his San Francisco gallery, but he gave him advice, and even traded one of his photographic prints for one of the boy's woodblock prints. While in San Francisco, Everett apparently enjoyed a brief romance with a girl named Frances.

In his biography of Everett, W. L. Rusho speculates that Everett, in the company of so many truly seasoned artists, might have experienced self-doubt about his own worth as an artist, and, sensing that he wasn't making progress, he returned home in the spring of 1934, where he began planning another trip to Arizona. Waldo offered to drive him there, dropping Everett off in Kayenta in April.

Everett spent time with the Navajo around Kayenta and Monument Valley and drifted north into Utah to climb Navajo Mountain and visit Rainbow Bridge, the largest natural stone bridge in the world. This was some of the emptiest wilderness Everett had yet encountered.

Everett hooked up with an archaeological team unearthing Anasazi and Basket Maker Indian remains in Tsegi Canyon. The leader of the dig, Clay Lockett, later told W. L. Rusho that Everett seemed less interested in archaeology than in looking at the scenery. Lockett also told the biographer that the youth took little heed for his own safety and almost killed himself climbing while trying to get into position to sketch a waterfall.

Everett seemed aware but unconcerned with his own recklessness, writing to an acquaintance from Monument Valley: "Hundreds of times I have trusted my life to crumbling sandstones and nearly vertical angles in the search for water or dwellings. Twice I was nearly gored to death by a wild bull. But always, so far, I've escaped unscathed and gone forth to other adventures." To another friend, he wrote, "One way and another, I have been flirting pretty heavily with death, the old clown."

After the Tsegi dig shut down, Everett traveled to the Hopi mesas in Arizona to witness a series of ceremonial dances. At Mishongnovi, his Hopi friends invited him to participate in one. Everett paid a surprise visit to Clay Lockett at his home in Flagstaff, went down to Sedona to paint the famous red cliffs of Oak Creek Canyon, and then moved on to the South Rim of the Grand Canyon at Desert View. He crossed over the Colorado River, probably at Marble Canyon, near Lees Ferry, making his way north across the Kaibab Plateau into Utah. By mid-October, he was enjoying the tourist overlooks at Bryce Canyon and living in the home of a park ranger. From there, Everett rode east toward the canyon tableau of the Escalante River country.

Everett rode into the tiny Mormon town of Escalante on his burro. He made friends easily with other young folk and found himself caught up in the town's social life. He was flattered by the attention, but in a letter to Waldo—the last known letter anyone ever received from him—Everett made it clear that this kind of social life was not suited to him. "I don't think I could ever settle down," Everett wrote to his brother. "I have known too much of the depths of life already, and I would prefer anything to an anticlimax." Everett left town on Armistice Day, riding southeast into the emptiness of the Kaiparowitz Plateau. A week later, he met up with a pair of sheepherders camped at Soda Gulch. They watched him depart two days later, bound for Hole in the Rock, near where the Escalante River joins the Colorado. There is no evidence that another living soul ever saw Everett Ruess again after that day.

To this day, no one knows what became of him. When Everett's parents failed to hear from their son in a timely manner, they alerted authorities, and the search for Everett was on. In some ways, that search has been going on ever since.

Everett's two burros were found corralled in Davis Gulch, a major side canyon to the Escalante. All his gear was missing, including his painter's kit and journal. Most baffling were two graffiti inscriptions that searchers found chiseled onto Indian ruins in the canyon. The first appeared at the base of a doorway on an Anasazi dwelling: NEMO 1934. A second Nemo inscription and the date was found on a ledge near some petroglyphs: Did Everett make these?

Everett's parents certainly thought so. *Nemo* is Latin for "no one." Everett's mother wrote to authorities that her son had read the *Odyssey* and was no doubt familiar with the scene where Odysseus escapes the Cyclops by telling the giant that his name is Nemo. It later dawned on Everett's father that Nemo was also the name of the submarine captain in *Twenty Thousand Leagues Under the Sea,* one of Everett's favorite books. W. L. Rusho noted that Captain Nemo's motto for the *Nautilus* could very well have been Everett's own: *Mobilis in mobile,* meaning "Mobile in a mobile element," or, "free in a free world."

The search party that set out from Escalante found many footprints, indicating that Everett had done some daredevil climbing, but no evidence that he had fallen. The Escalante

River, a creek really, was too shallow for anyone to drown in. Everett's size-nine boot prints led to the base of Fiftymile Mountain—perhaps he had climbed it and was then cut off by a heavy snowfall. But a thorough search of the bench and plateau west of the Colorado River revealed nothing. Rumors abounded that Everett had been killed by rustlers in Davis Gulch; that he was murdered by an outlaw Navajo named Jack Crank, who had bragged about killing a white man. But Everett's were the only footprints found in Davis Gulch. Theories that he had met with foul play were unsupported by any hard evidence.

A few believed Everett had pulled a vanishing act and was still alive. It was thought he might have crossed the Colorado River and gone to Monument Valley, and that he was hiding out among the Navajo. But no trace of him was found in Navajoland.

I think that it would have been out of character for Everett to stage his own disappearance. He was a loner, but hardly a recluse. He enjoyed people's company and made friends easily. And his letters reveal a genuine affection for his family. It is inconceivable to me that he would play so cruel a trick on them. Also inconceivable that he would abandon his art, his calling. Nonetheless, the romance that Everett went underground and is still out there persists to this day.

So what happened to Everett Ruess? One man who thinks he may have stumbled upon the answer is Ken Sleight, a wilderness outfitter from Moab, Utah, who has spent a considerable part of his life mulling over the Ruess legend and exploring the canyon country where Everett wandered. Sleight thinks Everett actually disappeared on the other side of the Colorado River, about forty miles east of the area where the original search party had been looking for him.

Over the years, Sleight, now in his late sixties, had explored the entirety of Davis Gulch, looking for clues that might explain Everett's disappearance. One day while investigating Grand Gulch, a canyon forty miles east of Davis Gulch, on the opposite side of the Colorado River, Sleight discovered the word *NEMO* scratched into an Anasazi ruin. Sleight couldn't be certain that Everett had made the inscription, but he thought it likely.

Here's what Sleight thinks might have happened: Everett corralled his burros in Davis Gulch and set out on foot, carrying all his supplies in his backpack. He forded the Colorado River at Hole in the Rock, then followed the Crossing of the Fathers, a trail blazed by Mormon pioneers. From that route, Everett could have descended into Grand Gulch to examine the Indian ruins and petroglyphs there. After leaving his Nemo mark in the stone, Everett could have hiked to the nearby San Juan River, only twenty miles north of his possible destination, Monument Valley. But Everett never made it to Navajoland. Sleight thinks Everett might have drowned while trying to ford the San Juan. I had plans to visit Sleight when I got to Moab, and I was looking forward to talking to him about Everett Ruess.

Obviously, we can't know Everett's last thoughts. One can only hope that his end came quickly. We can also hope Everett didn't experience overwhelming despair at the end or believe his life had come to nothing. For Everett could have had no way of knowing how his life and example were going to inspire people.

In 1940, Everett's mother arranged to have some of her sons letters and poems published in a book, *On Desert Trails With Everett Ruess*. The book soon went out of print and became a collector's item.

In the early 1980s, William Rusho, a Salt Lake City historian and chronicler of the Colorado Plateau, began piecing together Everett's story. His publisher, Peregrine Smith Books, had tracked down Everett's brother, Waldo, who agreed to make Everett's artwork and writings available for publication. Rusho traveled to places Everett had been, interviewing those who had known Everett or had participated in the search for the missing youth. Combining eyewitness accounts with Everett's essays, letters, and journals, he was able to put together a moving biography of the young artist, a story that the historian was able to tell primarily in Everett's own words.

It strikes me as remarkable that anyone as young as Ruess could write as well as he did. Prodigies, who are rather common in music, are almost unheard of in literature. Everett's essays are rhetorically over the top, and his journal entries are too dry and uninspirational to make interesting reading. But his letters to his family and friends, much more conversational in tone, come alive in their descriptive detail. He was an outstanding expository writer and he knew how to handle narrative well. A great sense of the desert Southwest is conveyed in Everett's prose. It's hard to imagine an American teenager today writing anything so lively, sharp, or well crafted. I looked at the black-and-white woodblock prints reproduced in Rusho's book. They were really very striking. There's no telling what this young man might have achieved had he lived long enough to develop his talents fully.

The youth who hungered after art but never personal fame became famous not only for the mystery surrounding his death but for his wholehearted dedication to the way he lived. Perhaps Everett's great good fortune was to find his theme early in life. He did things most of us only daydream about, giving up the comforts of home and casting off conformity, seeking adventure and hardship in unexplored lands. No doubt Everett lived life on a level too intense for most of us. If his naïveté could be charming, at times it could also be a little hard to take. Here was a boy who could practically swoon over a landscape and gush, "I have seen almost more beauty than I can bear." But his spirit and example are inspirational.

In *The Monkey Wrench Gang*, Hayduke, after disabling a diesel engine, scrawls his signature N E M O in the sand. The novelist John Nichols, in his introduction to Rusho's biography of Ruess, concluded that Everett's life was his greatest work of art. And in *Mormon Country*, Wallace Stegner had this to say about the young vagabond artist:

> *What Everett was after was beauty, and he conceived beauty in pretty romantic terms. We might be inclined to laugh at the extravagance of his beauty-worship if there were not something almost magnificent in his single-minded dedication to it. Esthetics as a parlor affectation is ludicrous and sometimes a little obscene; as a way of life it sometimes attains dignity. If we laugh at Everett Ruess we shall have to laugh at John Muir, because there was little difference between them except age.*

The story of Everett Ruess is about more than desert romance and a mysterious vanishing. It is about one artist's relationship to the earth and the desire to live life on a simpler, deeper level. And it is about personal freedom and a wilderness constantly revealing itself to us. Rusho said in his biography that to tell Everett's story was to render the landscape itself. In his day, few people understood him. Today, his idealism inspires more people than it confounds, and there is a greater acceptance of Everett's wilderness ethic and aesthetic.

Very few visitors to Utah venture into the actual backcountry. Most confine themselves to the national parks. I drove fifty-seven miles through a massive slickrock desert southeast of Escalante on a little-improved track called the Hole in the Rock Road. I found a world of slickrock. I was only a few miles from Davis Gulch, Everett's last known camp. I had followed the trail of the remarkable teenager who had wandered among earth's most panoramic places and had come to rest near here, in a side canyon of the Escalante, in what is perhaps the most remote region in the lower forty-eight. I cut the engine and looked about. The Fiftymile Bench and Kaiparowitz Plateau rose at my back. Ahead of me were Escalante's finger canyons. From where I stood, there was little evidence that this great ocean of slickrock had changed much since Everett's day.

It's tempting to give in to the fantasy that Everett Ruess still hides out here somewhere. On one level, we want to know what happened to him; on another, we want the mystery to go on. The legend of Everett Ruess will endure as a dream of youthful idealism and romantic individualism. People will go on searching for him and puzzling over him and trying to find exactly where he died. But in another sense, we know where Everett Ruess can be found. All we have to do is walk out into the immensity of the desert country he loved so well and we will find him waiting for us. He is everywhere under our feet.

7

UNCHARTED TERRAIN

I PITCHED A TENT in the uninhabited immensity of the Escalante benchlands. This was what I had been looking for. After the crowded national parks, here was true wilderness. This was also our nation's newest national monument. In 1996, over the howls of Congress, President Clinton had used his executive fiat to create in one fell swoop a new national monument called the Grand Staircase–Escalante. (It was a cynical act; Clinton was courting the environmental vote for the upcoming presidential election.) The monument is 1.7 million acres in size and encompasses the cliffs of the Grand Staircase, the Kaiparowitz Plateau, and the Escalante canyons. The new monument borders on Bryce, Glen Canyon National Recreation Area, and Canyonlands National Park. A mind-numbingly huge chunk of backcountry, totally undeveloped. Here are great distances, an enormously difficult terrain, and a remoteness rarely equaled in the United States outside of Alaska. With a backcountry permit, issued free in the town of Escalante, you can camp just about anywhere in the monument. No-trace camping is the rule in the backcountry. It might sound as if political correctness has come even to the desert, but the no-trace rule means sweeping up footprints and marks from the tent pad, refluffing stomped vegetation, and carrying out everything that has been carried in, including biodegradables, which I presume means human waste. (I buried mine six inches under the ground and burned the bum wad.) No-trace also means camping five hundred feet from any Jeep trail and completely out of sight of other campers. Diehards suggest not wearing bright colors, which might distract others, but that's giving fanaticism a bad name.

What grandeur and desolation lay out there. From rocky rim to world's end, the light burned on an emptiness of sky and desert. It seemed to be a world just ending—or just beginning. The land spread outward in stone wrinkles and incomprehensible strata. Down there in the rock labyrinths were canyon streams brightly snaking their way toward the Escalante River. Salmon pink cliffs rose out of a sea of stony waves. In the distance floated the Henry Mountains, five gray-green peaks high above the heat waves. Ellen, Pennell, Hillers, Holmes, and Ellsworth—the last five mountain peaks to be discovered in the contiguous United States.

Maj. John Wesley Powell, the one-armed Civil War veteran, had named them, coming down the Colorado. Powell discovered and named the Dirty Devil River, too, last unknown river in the lower forty-eight. (Unknown, unnamed, and undiscovered by everyone except the Indians, of course, who had known about them for centuries.) There it was, the river skirting the Henry Mountains and pouring into the Colorado, a wholly unexpected sight for a white explorer like Powell. It was 1869, the Civil War was over, peace blessed the republic, and the map of the United States territories still had a great blank area south and west of Denver.

In the past, travelers trying to settle the United States had avoided the largely impassable Colorado Plateau. For eons, powerful rivers had been at work on the plateau, carving out a twisting maze in the jumbled rock. Few had ventured into the inhospitable land of red canyons and fantastically eroded desert—and with good reason. The first Europeans to see the Grand Canyon were the Spanish conquistadors. They took one look into the abyss, turned tail, and fled. For the next two centuries, the Grand Canyon was written off as a route for exploration. Even by Powell's day, these badlands remained terra incognita.

Powell was going to explore and measure the Colorado Plateau and the Grand Canyon and fill in the map of the United States. His expedition launched in the summer of 1869 at Green River Station, Wyoming, the Union Pacific Railroad depot nearest the Colorado River system. An unlikely crew accompanied him—among them, a boy still in his teens, a newspaper editor, a man driven to mental breakdown in a Confederate prison, a disgruntled frontier army sergeant, a man hiding from the law, and an Englishman seeking adventure. Eight drifters and a boy led by a man with only one arm. Major Powell's right arm had been amputated after a minié ball shattered it at the Battle of Shiloh, and no one was quite sure just how Powell was going to be able to steer through rapids and climb steep canyon walls with only one hand to grab on with. Powell was a scientist in the grand Louis Agassiz tradition of the nineteenth century— that is, he was self-taught. An amateur in the best sense of the word, from the Latin *amator*, meaning "lover." His expedition was about to undertake what no one had dared before (not even the Indians, who lacked the necessary watercraft). Powell's men were going to float into the bowels of the red plateau, a journey of one thousand miles, starting at where the Green River heads in Wyoming and ending (if they survived) at the outlet of the Grand Canyon, where the Virgin River empties into the Colorado River.

They passed into territory that was almost wholly uncharted and little known or understood. Down the Green, born in the snowmelt of the Wind River Range in Wyoming; through Flaming Gorge in Utah; past the dinosaur beds of Echo Park; through the Gates of Lodore; down the canyon Powell named Desolation; emerging out the pink door of the Book Cliffs; and there to drift across the Green River desert into yet more canyons; finally coming to the confluence with the Grand, as that branch of the Colorado was known in Powell's day; there to float past the Land of Standing Rocks and into the peace of Glen Canyon; and then lastly to drift into the greatest wonder of them all, the Grand Canyon.

They were presented with what was perhaps the best river ever to flow through the United States. The Colorado wound like a fugue through the paramount landscape of the West. Its currents carried Powell's crew into one of the greatest adventures in the American canon. Theirs was a theme as bold as the republic itself: a celebration of the common man; rebels and misfits as heroes; freedom and self-reliance; romantic escape and grand adventure. The essential quality of America resided in its unsettled wilderness. That's what James Fenimore Cooper had been writing about in his *Leatherstocking Tales*. The American wilderness was a blank page, where an individual could write his destiny large. The frontier helped form the national character, avowed the historian Frederick Jackson Turner, and it became a primal source of democracy. And the promise of the frontier was like the promise of democracy itself: that its riches would always be there to spend.

With frontier optimism, our war hero approached Congress for support for his "scientific expedition." With their usual keen foresight, the nation's representatives showed Powell the door. But Powell's friend General Grant, soon to become president, promised rations for Powell's crew.

Exploration of the Colorado River of the West and Its Tributaries by John Wesley Powell is literary sleight of hand. You will have to read the actual journals that Powell and his men kept to find out exactly what transpired on that first expedition. Powell lost most of his notes and instruments due to mishaps on that first trip, and he had to do the whole expedition over again two years later in order to get the measurements and data right. Powell used that information along with many incidents and adventures from both expeditions and, for literary purposes, blended both voyages into one, using the cast of characters from his first trip. His narrative, first published in magazines and then as a book, and containing a few minor stretchers, was a best-seller.

Powell had a descriptive flare for naming places and landmarks. Unlike the geologist Clarence Dutton, who would follow Powell soon afterward and name many of the monoliths in the Grand Canyon after eastern mysticism, classical mythology, or Egyptian lore, Powell relied on a splendid form of frontier poetry for his place names.

He christened a foul-smelling tributary of the Colorado the Dirty Devil River. As a counterpoint, a delightful little stream in the Grand Canyon became Bright Angel Creek. An Edenic garden of greenery in the Grand Canyon was named Elves Chasm and another Vasey's Paradise after a botanist friend of his who would never get to see it. Rouge limestone formations gave birth to the Redwall Cavern in the Grand Canyon. Where Utah's Green River cut a startling red gorge into the landscape, Powell came up with the perfect name: Flaming Gorge. Music Temple and Cathedral in the Desert were the names given to stunning alcoves in the peaceful canyon that he had named Glen. Separation Rapids would memorialize the spot where three members of Powell's crew abandoned the expedition and later perished at the hands of Shivwits Indians after climbing out onto the North Rim plateau of the Grand Canyon. We can only be grateful that Powell didn't follow the custom of his day and name everything he saw after crooked U.S. politicians. The only truly exotic tag pinned on the landscape was the Gates of Lodore, named by Powell's teenage boatman, Andy Hall. Andy was a Huck Finn following the frontier tide, a mule skinner and bullwhacker by age thirteen. Powell chanced upon the cheerful youth, then eighteen, at Green River, Wyoming, where he made Andy a last-minute addition to his crew. Andy might have spent his adolescence stepping in cow manure, but he named the Gates of Lodore after lines he had memorized in a Robert Southey poem. The kid was living proof that the frontier could produce remarkable paradoxes.

John Wesley Powell's voyage down the Colorado entered the mythology of wilderness exploration. His book and daring adventures had catapulted him to the kind of fame even Congress couldn't ignore. The soldier turned scientist organized the United States Geological Survey, where he was to begin the immense job of creating high-standard maps of the entire United States. Powell's goal was nothing less than the marriage of science and government. He worked hard to operate his bureau strictly on a scientific basis, and he resisted political pressures, which did not set well with Congress. As a result, Powell became embroiled in the great bureaucratic wars over the development of the West. There was a long tradition of eastern money interests selling the romance of the West to rubes. "Rain follows the plow" was a slogan used to gull farmers into moving into arid lands that could not be cultivated. Powell argued that the dream of westward expansion had to be tempered by scientific reality, especially when it came to the kind of limited development the arid West could sustain. His words fell on deaf ears in Congress. Powell, who put his faith in science, hadn't counted on politics, and he woefully underestimated his enemies. He particularly failed to guard himself against those congressmen from the western states who were furious that a lone bureaucrat was holding up manifest destiny. Powell was unprepared for their ad hominem attacks. The pro-expansionists waged a vicious campaign against Powell, attacking not only his credibility but also his integrity. Powell was ultimately hounded from office, and he disappeared—to retirement on the coast of Maine, about as far as one could get from the Grand Canyon.

It wasn't to be the last time Congress would dishonor the name of John Wesley Powell. When Glen Canyon Dam was built almost a century later, constricting the Colorado River like a tourniquet, the reservoir that backed up and drowned 186 miles of canyon land in Arizona and Utah was named Lake Powell. You couldn't commit a greater sacrilege if you had spray-painted the word *fuck* onto the ceiling of the Sistine Chapel. Gone was Glen Canyon, with its fantastic trellis of side canyons and narrow, vaulted grottoes. Gone were Music Temple and Cathedral in the Desert. Gone were Mystery Canyon and Labyrinth Canyon. Water has now even backed up to Rainbow Bridge, largest natural stone bridge on the planet. Also submerged was Ruess Arch in Davis Gulch where Everett chiseled NEMO onto the rocks. Glen Canyon Dam might well be the single worst environmental mistake in the history of the republic. Wave good-bye to the lost worlds of the Colorado Plateau.

A HALF-MOON ROSE over a shadowed and spiky landscape. The rocks and even the air took on a milky clarity. I could see for miles in the harsh and stony desert. The desert itself made for a kind of lunar landscape, coldly compelling. The ground was hard and cold and everything was grand and supremely indifferent. Somewhere out there, the poisonous datura, or jimson-weed, was offering up its creamy white flowers to the moon. Great horned owls called out. Ringtail cats and coyotes had left their rocky dens in search of prey. I could feel the promise of another, more primal world out there.

I awoke somewhere in the shank of night. The moon was down and the constellations had turned toward unfamiliar positions. The Big Dipper looked slightly askew. Here was the night sky as I had rarely seen it, a limpid river of glittering stars bending to the horizons. Was that blue letter *W* Cassiopeia? The stars gleamed in numbers beyond anything I could remember. We live in a world of television sets and freeway overpasses and the Internet, but when we are born, and again when we die, we must come to a place very much like this, of desert and stars.

By looking up into the starry night above me, I was looking into time. I was actually seeing the past. The optical binary I saw within the scales of Libra—the brighter of the pair, sixty-five light-years distant—showed the star as it actually existed in the year before Everett Ruess's disappearance. The light from Schedar, a bright star burning in Cassiopeia, was the star as it existed on those nights when John Wesley Powell slept beside the banks of the Colorado on his second expedition. And that same star Powell viewed 126 light-years distant was light burning at the time of the original thirteen colonies. Surely the night sky overhead was showing me a few stars as they existed when the Anasazi lived in this desert. And they must have looked upon a midnight that showed stars burning when their ancestors crossed the Bering land bridge.

Everything came out of those stars. We are carbon life-forms descended from exploded bits of outer space, galactic dust that blew here on the stellar storms. We are molecules in a DNA continuum that had its source in the big bang of space and time. Did a divine power create all this, or is creation itself the divine power? Like a proper philosopher, I rolled over in the sack and tried to get back to sleep. Let someone else access the limits of perplexity.

8

A WRINKLE IN THE EARTH

ONE OF THE BEST things about the primitive Calf Creek Campground is that the host almost never turns anyone away. When
it fills up, latecomers are allowed to camp in an adjacent area
as scenic as the campground itself. The thirteen-site tent ground
is run by unpaid volunteers from the Bureau of Land Management, an agency usually associated with mismanaging our
western public lands. But these volunteers do a splendid job
maintaining the little BLM campground, which gets very
crowded in late spring and summer. The attraction is Calf
Creek Falls, the most popular hike in the monument. Its popularity is due, no doubt, to the fact that Calf Creek is close by
one of only two asphalt roads that pass through the huge Grand
Staircase–Escalante monument lands. Highway 12 runs between the little towns of Escalante and Boulder and was built
by the Civilian Conservation Corps back in 1938. FDR's CCC
was well intentioned but inaptly named, as it probably did
more to harm the environment than can be calculated. Until the
two-lane blacktop, mail and supplies were packed in to the
town of Boulder by mules and horses over Hell's Backbone

Road. Boulder has the distinction of being the last town in the United States to be serviced by mule-train delivery.

I wanted to see the waterfall and I wanted to fish for wild trout in a canyon of red-and-cream Navajo sandstone. Spring-fed Calf Creek flows cold and clear on its way to the Escalante. Not many streams in the Utah desert hold trout. Calf Creek is brimming with them year-round. European brown trout were planted in this creek more than a century ago, and while they could not be considered native to the stream, they were wild and plentiful, if not large.

The sandstone walls were full of solution holes, scouring depressions hollowed out by wind and rain. I noticed a small miniature arch not far from the trailhead, formed over the millennia by the corrosive action of wind and water. Piñon pines bore the scars of hungry porcupines. The Indians who once made this canyon home, both the Anasazi and the earlier Fremont culture, made good use of what little there was here. Piñon nuts were a dietary staple, the rabbitbrush and hollygrape became a source of vegetable dyes, and the hard little berries of the juniper trees could be fashioned into primitive jewelry. No doubt the Indians grew melons in the bottomland, as did the Mormon farmers who came after them. I spotted one of those thousand-year-old Indian granaries, perched high on a canyon cliff, not far below the rim.

All along the trail were prickly pear cacti, blooming yellow and wine red. It had been a remarkable spring for desert wildflowers, thanks to El Niño. The wildflowers were everywhere, sprays of orange, blue, and yellow. The cactus blooms were the most beautiful. The shallow roots of the cacti absorbed water during brief rainy periods and their prickly pads stored it up for the long dry periods.

All this Navajo sandstone had formed millions of years ago, the result of ancient sand dunes. In nature, energy is constant, but the forms are shifting. Black streaks hung like drapes on the ham pink walls. This blue-black patina known as desert varnish was oxidized iron and manganese leached out by rainwater mixing with organic material. The desert varnish made a fine canvas for Indian petroglyphs. Petroglyphs are designs scratched out of rock, and pictographs are scenes or symbols painted onto the rock with pigments—the Anasazi used both art forms. For the petroglyphs, they scratched away at the desert varnish, exposing the redrock beneath it, so the red designs appear against a darker canvas. I stopped to admire some of this artwork on the smooth sandstone, maybe a thousand years old.

The path through the canyon followed a gentle stream banked by cheatgrass and horsetail. At last I came upon the waterfall, 126-feet high, plunging over the rim into a deep green pool and spraying a constant mist onto a mural of polished rock. A hanging garden of maidenhair ferns and monkey flowers clung to smooth walls streaked in running colors. The air was moist and freshened by the turbulence. The cooling interface between the air and the falling water was wonderful, and as I neared the pool, the air temperature around me dropped by twenty degrees.

I fly-fished my way back. The trout were utterly spooked by my presence. They scattered and darted for cover at my footfalls. The creek was so clear, you could count every trout in the stream. I have fly-fished all over the West and I have never encountered spookier trout than these. They were in constant terror of eagles and hawks patrolling the canyon.

I couldn't get close to them. I had to wade up the middle of the creek, hunched over, practically kneeling in the creek bed, casting directly upstream. Trout scattered before me—they had eyes in the backs of their heads. It was extremely frustrating. Finally, I fooled one stupid little brown trout into taking my fly. The trout couldn't have been more than five inches long. And yet it was one of the most brilliantly colored trout I have ever caught. I counted a dozen flaming red spots on its cold brown body. A truly beautiful little trout. Back in camp, I relaxed as evening came on. Chopped some wood for the fire. Admired the solution holes in the wall of red Navajo sandstone. From the bushes came a lovely, melodious chirping. Evening lingered and light fell through the clouds. Calf Creek made pleasant water noises nearby. Everything was peaceful and I was happy and satisfied.

MY CAR WOUND its way up the Boulder Mountain pass, climbing beyond nine thousand feet. It was freezing up here, the wind kicking up violent gusts. I had never seen so many aspens in one place. About half the stands had already leafed out and were shimmering golden green in the wind. The remainder of the trees, mostly growing on northerly slopes that received less sunlight, remained leafless, presenting a bare monochrome against the mountain. Here was the best view yet of the Henry Mountains to the east.

Capitol Reef isn't a reef any more than Bryce Canyon is a canyon. The red cliffs and high ridges rising up along the Waterpocket Fold were called "reefs" by Mormon pioneers, who found them a formidible barrier. Atop the red cliffs were whitish dome-shaped formations. These must have called up to the mind of some particularly dull person images of the Capitol dome in Washington, and that's how the place got its name. Sixty-five million years ago, when the Colorado Plateau was forming, the earth buckled up and folded into the landscape the way a carpet might bunch up if you were to push it against a wall. This ruck became known as the Waterpocket Fold, an immense wave of upturned sandstone one hundred miles long.

Capitol Reef is the high, eroded western edge of the crease. The name Capitol Reef might be a euphemism, but the water pockets were completely real. The sandstone landscape was pockmarked with stone pits and bowl-shaped depressions that filled up with water on the rare occasions that it rained out here. I stopped at Panorama Point to take in the vistas. From atop the Goosenecks, I had a great view of Sulphur Creek Canyon, with tiny hikers stepping daintily into the creek eight hundred feet below. Farther on in the park, I came upon a massive rock formation known as the Castle, a magnificent palisade flushed with warm desert colors. Chimney Rock appeared ready to topple. The Egyptian Temple, at the base of a great escarpment, resembled the contours of some wondrous edifice that might have been found in the valley of the Nile. Those ripple marks on the walls had been formed by lapping waves on tidal flats millions of years ago. When the earth's crust tilted upward, causing the shallow sea to shift, the subsequent uplifting, fracturing, and erosion left a scene of chaos—brown and redwall cliffs crowned by vaulted domes.

A stern warning sign was posted prominently at the entrance to Grand Wash: Hikers were cautioned not to enter the wash when storms were threatening. People had drowned in flash floods in these canyons. I looked and saw thunderheads on the western horizon. There was little breeze, but the black hammerheads of vapor were moving my way—that much was clear. I went into the wash anyway; I figured I had a couple of hours.

I walked the floor of the wash, alert for midget faded rattlers, which are known to frequent the area and which blend into the rocky terrain. My hike in the narrows gave me an indication of what a few flash floods could do to this canyon. Less than eight inches of rain falls annually, most of it during late summer thunderstorms. The twisting canyon was sheer-walled and deep, its facades polished to a brilliant finish. Water had cut a masterpiece out of this wash.

The Fremont Indians had been the first inhabitants here. Those ancient people had etched petroglyphs into the desert varnish covering the sandstone. Pictographs were less numerous. The Fremont, who inhabited Capitol Reef for about a thousand years, had left a record for us to try and decipher in our time—perhaps their bid for immortality.

I ignored the Cassidy Arch Trail, which led to a dugout somewhere in Grand Wash, the site of a hideout once said to have been used by Butch Cassidy and his Wild Bunch gang. Butch Cassidy was Utah's most famous jack Mormon. He had used Capitol Reef as a refuge and an escape route. These badlands had been made to order for his outlaws. They knew all the blind canyons and water holes. The Waterpocket Fold runs one hundred miles from Thousand Lake Mountain to the Colorado River and is a barrier that can be crossed in only a few spots, such as Grand Wash. The Wild Bunch used Capitol Reef as they moved from Brown's Hole to Robber's Roost and south on to New Mexico. As I said, I ignored the trail to Cassidy Arch. I once worked as a newspaper reporter, and frankly, I find bank robbers as banal as bank presidents.

Dark storm clouds were bunching up in the west, but the rain was still a ways off. The afternoon sun was beating directly over the hot wash and the wind was picking up. When I reached the end of the wash, where it comes out at the canyon of the Fremont River, I turned around for the two-mile hike back and found the wind in my face, which slowed my progress somewhat. Walking on loose sand into a headwind is a bitch. Although I wanted to explore a few of the narrow defiles in the wash, I decided not to linger.

Black clouds were massing by the time I retraced my steps

through Grand Wash. Dust devils were kicking up everywhere. It was going to get ugly. I drove to the campground at Fruita, when I hastily set up my tent, having great difficulty pounding the stakes into the hard, rocky ground. The sky was blackening over the park and everything looked about to let loose. The wind blew in strong, violent gusts. My tent began flapping wildly. I thought the stakes would pull out in the gale and the tent fly off. A few raindrops began to spatter, but no deluge. I could see slanting virgas of water appearing north of the park. Maybe the storm would skirt us.

Thunder rumbled and the wind howled. Gale-force gusts hit the camp. I was certain the tent was going to fly away. Still, no rain fell. We were going to miss the downpour. Slowly, the storm passed and the sky began to open up once again.

After an early supper, I took a walk down by the Fremont River. The campground was set down in a grove of orchards. Black-and-white swallows darted above the rushing river, snatching up hatching mayflies. I followed the path along the river's brushy banks. The stream appeared as a brownish turbulence, too muddy and warm to support trout.

I came upon the park amphitheater, situated in one of the orchard groves. The apricots were still green and rock hard. The original settlers in Fruita had planted these orchards, and their fruit trees flourished beside the Fremont River. The pioneers used essentially the same irrigation methods, a network of ditches, as did the Fremont Indians seven hundred years ago. The Mormons traded their fruit for grains and supplies, hauling their harvest to neighboring settlements by horse-drawn wagon. These days, the National Park Service manages the orchards, and in season tourists are invited to pick their fill of cherries, apricots, peaches, pears, and apples.

The Fremont River was named after the explorer John Charles Frémont, who had traveled in this wilderness in the

1850s. The Fremont is a tributary of the Dirty Devil River, last "undiscovered" river in the country. From its source in the mountains to the west, the Fremont cuts a course through the rock jumble known as the Waterpocket Fold, on its way to meet the Dirty Devil and the Colorado. The green riverine vegetation brought relief to the russet desert.

I noticed beaver scorings on the cottonwood trunks, yet the river was free of logjams. The current was too fast for the beavers to build dams, so they had to content themselves with hollowing out dens along the banks.

Beyond the orchards, a path led from a meadow, where deer browsed, out through an opening in the fence and onto a wide expanse of sagebrush. I followed the trail to the base of a high cliff, and began a long climb to the overlook.

Swallows wheeled and soared above the brown cliffs, snatching insects out of the air. The Moenkopi Formation rose up on both sides of the canyon, as distinct as a chocolate layer cake. I ran my hand over the rock to feel its smoothness. The trail led me up the face of the Moenkopi wall, now radiant in the glow of the setting sun. Once on top, I found the path led around to the backside of the cliff, and I scrambled up some switchbacks, coming out at a rock cairn that marked the trail's end.

I took a long drink from my canteen. Sundown filled the Fremont Canyon with a golden luminosity. A world of color met my eyes. Far below, the Fremont River snaked through its green orchards, bound for the hot colors of the redrock desert. Chocolate brown cliffs rose out of the valley, topped by red, then sugar white sandstone. The Moenkopi Formation was simple to pick out, so distinctive in its chocolate shading. Immediately above appeared a grayish green band with streaks of maroon, known as the Chinle Formation. Above the Chinle was a dramatic sight—a sheer wall of red-orange sandstone 350 feet high, blazing back in the sunset. This was the Wingate sandstone, and I could see those places where erosion from the softer, underlying Chinle had caused entire blocks of the Wingate to drop away into space, leaving behind sheer vertical walls streaked by desert varnish. Here was a canvas for some of the finest Indian rock art in the Americas.

The Wingate cliffs above Fruita are filled with petroglyphs and pictographs, designs painted or chiseled a thousand years ago. Most unusual are the "anthromorphs"—human shapes with bucket heads and trapezoidal torsos. These apparitions wear elaborate headgear that includes dangling ear bobs and necklaces, and their short arms and legs do not match their oversize trunks. So abstract and bizarre did they appear that some whites at first mistook them for images left behind by ancient astronauts. And there are other designs on the rocks: handprints, bighorn sheep, and the occasional Kokopelli figure, a hunchbacked spirit flautist who was said to be older even than Yahweh, and who led his people out of the third world of existence into the present one.

Modern Indians, like the Hopi, understand what the images signify. The presence of the anthromorphs, they say, indicates that important rituals were conducted nearby. Other symbols mark clan migrations or seasonal planting schedules.

I picked out a boulder to sit on. A light breeze blew steadily around me. I listened to a steady chirp of birds, a faint hum of insects. There can be no such thing as silence up here. No such thing as silence anywhere, not even in the stillness that accompanies a great solitude. In this life, we can't know what real silence is. Even our blood makes a continuous sound in our ears.

9

RIMROCK WORLD

AN EXTRAORDINARY DRIVE north from Capitol Reef. On my right, bare stone, salmon pink tablelands gouged out by the unseen Green and Colorado rivers. On my right, the San Rafael Swell, a rugged wilderness rising fifteen hundred feet above the desert floor, a giant uplifted dome of sedimentary rock, one of the wonders of southern Utah. A backpacker's paradise, riddled with slot canyons, jagged cliffs, and valleys so deep that only the intrepid set out to explore them. The San Rafael Swell had been proposed—off and on—for consideration as a national park. I wasn't about to hold my breath waiting for that to happen.

But the tableland on my right *was* a national park, Canyonlands. It had been created in 1964 and was perhaps the least "improved" park in the national system. Which made it the best, as far as I was concerned. Fewer tourists make it out to Canyonlands. There is little water, hardly any pavement, and absolutely nothing you might mistake for an NPS amenity. It is incredibly tough to get into—you have to drive forever. Most tourists stop in nearby Arches National Park, which is very crowded; fewer make the effort to reach Canyonlands. People don't know what they are missing, and that was fine with me. I was headed for Island in the Sky, a huge mesa that makes up a third of Canyonlands National Park. At the ranger station, a sign warned NO WATER, NO GAS, NO ELECTRICITY. No services of any kind up on the mesa.

What a landscape. I drove over the Neck, a narrow isthmus of rock providing the only possible access for cars venturing onto the high mesa. Early cowboys once fenced the Neck to make the entire island an inescapable grazing land for their cattle. Erosion is at work on the Neck, and some day it will wear away to nothing. Then there will be no way to get up on the mesa, unless it is with pitons and crampons.

It was a long drive through Grays Pasture. At the road junction, a turnoff to the right led to Upheaval Dome and the Green River Overlook, but I ignored this and kept heading south. The asphalt ran out at Grandview Point, a gnarled finger of land jutting out from Island in the Sky, the very tip of the mesa pointing out toward the confluence of the Colorado and Green rivers. Most tourists lingered by the parking lot overview; fewer followed the trail over slickrock leading out for half a mile to a great promontory where the mesa finally ends. There are four grand scenic backdrops in the United States, places where your jaw drops and you say to yourself, *This is it.* Places where it looks as if God blew his entire budget for the creation. These four are the Grand Canyon, Big Sur on the California coast, the Grand Tetons in Wyoming, and this view from the promontory of Grandview Point in Utah. Oddly, while nearly everyone is familiar with the first three vistas, relatively few have ever seen or heard of the last.

I followed a trail of rock cairns over a massive outcropping of sandstone and climbed to a lofty overhang where I could look out over the brink of everything and nothing. I was spellbound, drawn into the void. Beneath my feet, the mesa wall dropped, twelve hundred feet, straight down to a wide shelf of creamy sandstone known as the White Rim bench. Beyond the White Rim, a second cliff plummeted fifteen hundred feet and more to the Colorado River, unseen from my vantage. Two giant steps: from the top of the mesa to the bottom of the gorge.

On my left was the corkscrew trench of the Colorado; on my right, the deep defile of the Green River. Junction Butte rose before me like a thundercloud hardened into sandstone, and beyond it and far below the White Rim lay the crack in the rock where, somewhere down there unseen, the Green and Colorado merge. Just beyond the confluence was the spiny stone wilderness named the Needles; west of the junction were the orange-banded canyon labyrinths known as the Maze. The air was absolutely clear and the views went on into infinity. Beyond the mesas were mountains, the Abajos to the south, the snowcapped La Sals toward Colorado, and the Henrys to the southwest, interrupting the horizon.

This could have been a world just forming, or just coming to its end. The sun was hot, the canyon colors hotter yet: reds, browns, and orange-banded rock, with little in the way of green to relieve the panorama. A stunning world of shape rose in colored bands. I looked out upon ten thousand square miles of stark landscape, a wizard's realm, the likes of which exist nowhere else on earth. Here lay a dozen major canyons, gouged and corkscrewed, and hundreds of minor ones, most permanently dry. I could not count the number of mesas, buttes, spires, pinnacles, domes, knobs, towers, natural arches, stone bridges, and overhangs out there.

Grandview Point—the view was grand indeed. From my rock, I was exposed to an almost 180-degree panorama. I stared down at the chocolate-colored hoodoos and capstones of Monument Basin below the White Rim. Looking south, across the terraced barriers of the Colorado River, I saw the Needles, a crenelated castlement, the orange-banded spires changing tone with each passing cloud. Steep-walled valleys known as the Grabens lay beyond. I made out the white-humped back of Elephant Hill and the heaved-up blocks of the Devils Kitchen. Somewhere in that deep jumble were the fingers of Horse and Salt Creek canyons, with their Indian ruins and pictographs. Down there lay a few water-cut canyons with life-giving springs, and other stranger canyons through which no stream has ever flowed.

Beyond the confluence, I saw the Land of Standing Rocks, where the Maze begins. There were Ernies Country and the Fins and the striped minarets of the Doll House. I made out Chimney Rock and, farther out, Bagpipe Butte and Teapot Rock and the Orange Cliffs behind them; and across the deep defile of the Green River, I spied the magnificent Turks Head, the Buttes of the Cross, and my very favorite rock, Cleopatras Chair, a slanting throne, which at that moment was illuminated by a golden shaft of sunlight escaping out of the clouds.

My eyes were lost in the orange Maze, where multicolored walls kept repeating themselves. The sheer canyons here twist and turn in all directions, dividing and subdividing into an ever-confusing labyrinth. In the Land of Standing Rocks, eroded towers, slender fins of stone, and massive buttes stand above and among these twisting orange canyons.

In order to get to the Maze, I would have had to climb down from Island in the Sky and swim across the Green River. Or I would have had to leave Island in the Sky and drive all the way back to Hanksville, a journey of more than a hundred miles. To visit the Needles, I would have had to drive down from the mesa, leave the park, and travel well south of Moab; or climb down the White Rim, ford the Colorado River, and then climb up the Talus Rim. Everywhere, these tablelands had been cut by deep, impassable canyons, and the three biggest converged into a Y-shaped abyss formed by the confluence of the Green and Colorado rivers.

The stupendous ravines that form the Y divide Canyonlands into three distinctive sections: the Maze, the Needles, and the Island in the Sky. Grandview Point is on the jutting tip of the latter, high above the merging rivers. The mesa is indeed an island that rises out of an ocean of fantastic rock.

I sat on the overhang at Grandview Point for a few hours, taking in agoraphobic views of convoluted canyons, grand cliffs and mesas, and rusty deserts in between and beyond. Somehow, I managed to tear myself away for a few hours to backtrack and explore a few other choice sections of the mesa, such as Upheaval Dome, the Green River Overlook, and Mesa Arch Trail.

A short hike through a piñon and juniper woodland on the mesa's eastern edge took me out to Mesa Arch, a span of Navajo sandstone hanging precariously near the edge of a cliff. The arch was like a picture frame, with a striking view of the La Sal Mountains thirty-five miles to the east. Directly below me was the White Rim and Buck Canyon and the even deeper gorge of the Colorado River. Looking out through the arch, I could see another smaller arch farther away, on the left, Washer Woman, so named because it resembles a woman leaning over a tub. The large pinnacle close by the right of Washer Woman was Monster Tower, and the isolated butte farther out, behind Washer Woman, was Airport Tower.

Walking out on the trail, I had noticed a dark gray crust on the soil. This powdery coating is cryptobiotic crust, a plant colony of microscopic lichens, algaes, mosses, and fungi. The crust makes a kind of delicate skin on the desert, acting as both a protective covering and a binding agent for future plant life, retarding erosion, absorbing moisture, and producing nitrogen.

Not much to look at, but the basis of life in the desert. A seed falling into cryptobiotic soil is more likely to survive than one falling onto sterile sand. In some ways, the crust is tough stuff—fully capable of weathering the scorching sun, rainstorms, and freezing cold. But it cannot withstand a hiking boot or the tires of a mountain bike. People are asked to stay on the trails and keep off the stuff. It might take fifty years or more for a thin patch of soil to develop; one footstep could wipe out years, even decades, of nature's work.

I went out to the Green River Overlook to take in the magnificent views of the Green River winding serenely under the White Rim. I admired the Turks Cap, a capstone of whitish rock once a part of the White Rim and now cut off and isolated by a bend in the river. On July 17, 1869, Maj. John Wesley Powell and his men floated below this viewpoint on their way to the confluence of the two great rivers.

From here, I could see the brown-and-green edges of Upheaval Dome. This fifteen-hundred-foot crater on the western edge of Island in the Sky is a puzzle. Some think it was the sight of a meteor impact. Others believe that a half-mile underlying bed of salt left by an ancient sea rose like a bubble that ballooned and cracked open at the top layers of the earth.

I hiked back out to Grandview Point to enjoy the final moments of daylight. Long shadows crept into the creases of the rocks, giving even greater drama to the rugged terrain. The colors of the blue mesas, orange towers, and maroon stacks intensified in the setting sun and whole mounds of earth seemed to be disappearing into a violet haze.

I spent the night at Willow Flat, a dry, primitive campground. No water whatsoever—I drank what I had brought with me in my car. And I needed the water badly; this climate can dehydrate a person quickly. Only a few crude and waterless campgrounds exist up here. It was very clear to me that this landscape didn't care if I lived or died. Nature is not a sentimentalist. Humans are of no more importance to the earth than bacteria. Everything is of equal value and of no value out here. Nature takes us all in with an unblinking stare.

10

SLICKROCK CAPITAL

EARLY THE FOLLOWING morning, I drove out to Pack Creek Ranch to see Ken Sleight. Ken's ranch is on a three-hundred-acre spread fourteen miles south of Moab, at the base of the La Sal Mountains. Mount Tukuhnikivatz, at more than twelve thousand feet, loomed over the scene. Its Ute name means "the place where the sun lingers longest." Heading in, I spied a lane on my left, its street sign reading ABBEY'S ROAD. On the right, another sign said TAKE THE OTHER. There was a third blacktop lane marked by yet another sign: SELDOM SEEN ROAD.

In his novel *The Monkey Wrench Gang*, Edward Abbey based the character Seldom Seen Smith on his good friend Ken Sleight. In and around Moab, Sleight has a reputation for impertinence. He is not your typical Utah Mormon businessman.

Sleight pioneered what today would be regarded as the modern version of white-water river running and canyoneering. Sleight began running rivers commercially in 1951, the year I was born. He was one of a lucky handful to see Glen Canyon, taking his rafts through it, before it was drowned under Lake Powell. He has run the Grand Canyon, Cataract and Westwater canyons on the Colorado, most of the canyons on the Green River, and the San Juan. As a horse packer and hiker, he explored the little-known backcountry of Grand Gulch, Dark Canyon, Coyote Canyon, and the Maze. He combed every inch of Davis Gulch and the Escalante Canyon, looking for clues that might explain the disappearance of Everett Ruess. Sleight is a canyon-country veteran who has bridged the old and new eras. A radical environmentalist, he, too, had to have his consciousness raised. In bygone days, like other guides from the old school, he used to throw his beer cans into the river and his Tootsie Roll wrappers on the trail.

Pack Creek Ranch seemed to fit into a style somewhere between country chic and bunkhouse primitive. No phones or TVs in the guest cabins. When they started this place, Ken and his wife, Jane, wanted to create something of a country inn and guest ranch—not exactly a dude ranch—but a place where guests could come to enjoy white-water and canyon adventures, saddle up horses, hike into the mountains—or do nothing at all. Edward Abbey used to come out here to write, holing up in Road House Cabin. The ranch has a splendid setting: to the west the redrock cliffs behind Moab; to the east, rolling hills and flats of prickly pear and juniper rising up gently into the La Sals.

A fresh mountain breeze rustled the cottonwoods and thunder rumbled in the distance. Three black cats played in the driveway between Meadow House and the Bunk House. In the office just off the dining room, under wagon-wheel chandeliers, a table display proffered complete sets of Edward Abbey's books. There were other books, too—an eclectic selection, mostly volumes of regional interest on the Colorado Plateau— casually arranged on bookshelves in a makeshift library with a fieldstone fireplace. The dining room had just been cleared of breakfast plates.

Ken Sleight approached with an extended hand, a coffee mug in the other. "Jane's not here today," he said. "She's up in Wyoming right now." Hawk-faced, lanky, his eyes accented by crinkled laugh lines. "Do you want breakfast? . . . No? Then let's go over to my office." His office was a cinder-block bunker crammed with file boxes dating back to the 1940s.

"I'm supposed to be writing my memoirs," Sleight said, with the resignation of a man not looking forward to a session with the typewriter. I commented on the file boxes and their dates. "The University of Utah has asked me to donate my papers. I have to go through all this stuff."

I asked him if he was pleased with the creation of Grand Staircase–Escalante National Monument. Most people in Utah opposed the new monument and were angrier than hell over the manner in which it had been created—by presidential fiat. I had thought Sleight would be for it, because it would put the wilderness out of the reach of commercial developers.

"It'll be the worst thing to happen since Glen Canyon Dam," Sleight said flatly, an answer that surprised me. "You build a road, and it begets another road, which begets a trail, which begets a rest stop and a toilet, and before you know it, everything is developed." He said Grand Staircase–Escalante should be designated properly as an official wilderness area so there can be absolutely no development within its borders. He said it still wasn't too late for Congress to act.

"I met Ed Abbey when he was a ranger at Lees Ferry," Sleight said, leaning back in his chair and propping a pair of well-worn cowboy boots on the desk. "He was checking our rafting permits. We stayed up until two in the morning, drinking and talking about how to get rid of Glen Canyon Dam. Ed had already written *Desert Solitaire,* from the time he was a ranger at Arches, and I told him how much I liked it. We shared a love and a feeling for this land."

Sleight said *The Monkey Wrench Gang* grew out of stories they swapped around campfires. "All that stuff showed up in the book," Sleight said. "Around the campfire, we'd work out these things, and then later, when I read the book, I found that he'd put it all down pretty much the way it was told. For instance, one day Ed asked me if you could winch a Jeep down a cliff."

I asked Sleight if it would physically be possible to pull off what occurred in that famous scene in the book, where Hayduke escapes Bishop Love's Search and Rescue vigilantes by winching his Jeep down a sheer precipice. Sleight just shrugged his shoulders in a "who knows" gesture and laughed. As for his own monkey-wrenching, Sleight called his desert night-riding escapades of the past "civil disobedience."

"The destruction of the wilderness was taking place right in front of our eyes," he said. Like most Utahans, Sleight is by nature independent. But unlike the majority of his fellow citizens, who welcomed development for commercial purposes, Sleight fought to preserve the canyon country. It made him odd man out in southeastern Utah, where environmentalists are generally resented and where the attitudes among many of Ken's fellow Utahans could largely be summed up in the words of Louise Liston, a Garfield County commissioner from Escalante, who liked to complain that backpackers visited the area with only a twenty-dollar bill in their pockets, the clothes on their backs, and wouldn't change either during their stay. For years, the people of Utah had been nice to these visitors, hauling them out of the sand when they'd get stuck, rescuing them from the canyons, and now these tenderfeet wanted to tell them how to run their lives. Ken said Utahans could be slow in coming around to the progressive viewpoint.

As we talked, Sleight would answer the ringing telephone and speak briefly to the people on the other end of the line. One lengthier call came from a friend who was recovering from cancer. Another call was from his friend Mark Maryboy, a San Juan County commissioner who represented the Navajo. Sleight, as concerned with issues of social justice as he is with the environment, had been working to change the county government to a council system with district representation— which would give the Navajo more of a voice in the local government. Sleight was a thorn in the side of the Republican-controlled political machine in San Juan County, and the "good old boy" establishment had recently blocked his appointment to the Economic Board.

"Did you say you were a trout fisherman?" Sleight asked me after he hung up the phone. "Mark Maryboy loves to fly-fish. I should get the two of you together."

Sleight wanted to talk about Glen Canyon. A few months earlier, he had hosted the spring meeting of the Glen Canyon Institute at Pack Creek Ranch, its goal to restore Glen Canyon by removing the infamous dam. More than one hundred people attended. Folk singer Katie Lee sang her river songs and read from her book *All My Rivers Are Gone*. Bill Wolverton, a ranger in Escalante, presented a slide show documenting natural restoration in Coyote, Fiftymile, and Davis gulches and Twilight Canyon following a corrective drawdown of the Lake Powell reservoir.

So disgusted was Sleight with the damming of Glen Canyon in the early 1960s that he said good-bye to Utah. "I was looking for something new," he said. He established a commercial outfitting business in Alaska and led rafting trips down the Yukon River. But after a few years, the redrock canyons called him back. "There are no canyons like these anywhere else on earth," Sleight said. "Somewhere along the line, you have to make a stand."

Sleight believes much of the wild has fled the Utah wilderness. That is why he has such strong feelings about opening up the Escalante canyons and Kaiparowitz Plateau as a tourist-friendly national monument, and why he fights to prevent such things as the paving of the Hole in the Rock Road and the Burr Trail and new marinas on Lake Powell.

"Wilderness is no longer there in the way we used to know it," Sleight said. "You could float down the river and never see another soul. Now we have mountain bikes all over Moab. You can't go out to the Shafer Trail [on the White Rim in Canyonlands] without getting run over by a Jeep. It's a little hard to handle."

Sleight acknowledged that he and his friend Abbey were partly responsible for all this. Abbey's books popularized the redrock canyon country and inspired many to visit Utah and Arizona—but they also helped evolve a new environmental consciousness.

"I'm part of the problem—we're all part of the problem," Sleight said. "I'm a businessman. And, as a businessman, you know when you're overstepping your bounds. As much as I can, I wrap my company around my environmental philosophy. Otherwise, I wouldn't do it."

Sleight said that his broad antiauthoritarian streak can be traced back to his having had to endure a strict Mormon upbringing. He was born in a small town in the Idaho desert and his family moved to Utah when he was ten. His love of the outdoors came out of his youthful experiences, when the wilderness was both an escape and a refuge for him.

"Wilderness to me is about freedom, and without wilderness, you can have no freedom. What inspires people to come out here is the natural beauty of the setting and the adventure and excitement. It puts meaning into your life."

I asked Sleight his theory about the disappearance of Everett Ruess, a favorite subject of his. Sleight has long been fascinated by the legend of the lost boy.

"I've been over every inch of the Escalante looking for some sign," Sleight said. "In Davis Gulch, you could find his footprints, if you knew where they were. One day, I was over in Grand Gulch on the San Juan River and I saw the word *Nemo* chiseled onto the rock of an Indian ruin. Now, I can't say for certain that Everett made this mark. But my guess is that he was on his way to visit his Navajo friends at Monument Valley. He left his mules corralled in Davis Gulch and crossed the Colorado at Hole in the Rock. From there, he took a side trip to Grand Gulch to look at the Indian ruins. He was playing his Nemo game, and he made that inscription on the rock. My guess is that he drowned while trying to cross the San Juan River."

I DROVE OUT to Arches after my morning with Ken Sleight. And I'm sorry to say it was much too crowded and too well maintained for me actually to enjoy it. Which was a pity, because this national park really is one of the most stunning places on earth. Here is the greatest concentration of natural arches in the world—two thousand cataloged, and still counting, some as miniature as three feet in length, others among the largest in the world. Standing in this playground of arches are spires, balanced rocks, freestanding fins, and eroded monoliths made up of rouge-colored Entrada sandstone. Nature sculpted all this out of one massive block of rock.

The gateway to Arches is six miles north of Moab and the paved highway leads past remarkable formations such as the Organ, Tower of Babel, and the red hoodoos known as the Three Gossips. A trickle of salty water shines way down in Courthouse Wash. There is Balanced Rock, perched on its inadequate pedestal. The snow-covered La Sals gleam in the eastern distance.

I hiked out to what is probably the most remarkable formation in the park, Landscape Arch, the most breathtaking stone arch in the world. Spanning 291 feet, Landscape was once thought to be the largest stone arch existent. And then geologists, armed with laser equipment, discovered that the far less spectacular Kolob Arch in Zion actually measures longer, at 310 feet. Leave it to scientists to take the magic out of everything. Grand Canyon isn't the deepest canyon; Landscape Arch isn't the longest. . . . But we know better. Like all the arches, Landscape is not the arch it used to be, nor will it be the same tomorrow. Its gap grows ever wider, its span ever thinner. At its weakest point, it is now only six feet thick. It is not long for this world. A large piece of it broke off not long ago, and its fresh splinters and shards lay all over the ground when I was there. I wanted to stand beneath its thin, flattened span, but the area underneath was roped off. A hundred feet off the ground, the arch seemed to stretch to an incredible distance, like a strand of taffy pulled to the breaking point.

I followed the trail beyond Landscape to Partition and Navajo arches and to the Devils Garden beyond and then retraced my steps. There were way too many people on the trail to make this experience wholly pleasurable. I can't emphasize this enough. A park like Arches really needs to be experienced in the off-season. One should make the effort to visit this place in the harshest of seasons—preferably when it is under a blanket of snow. Not that I want to keep people out of our national parks. I'm as democratic as the next fellow. Hey, I'm a liberal— I love humanity; it's people I can't stand.

I drove around to enjoy the gallery's other masterworks, such as Delicate Arch, another feature attraction, a remarkable stone sculpture squatting in solitary splendor on the lip of a deep sandstone bowl. There is really nothing delicate about this great bowlegged arch rising above a sea of slickrock, unless you take into account a spot on one of its legs that has worn almost completely through. Cowboys used to call this massive sixty-five-foot rise of salmon pink sandstone, with its suggestive shape, the Schoolmarm's Bloomers. The arch is all that remains of a massive sandstone wall that once stood here. To explain how all this happened, geologists like to draw an analogy to the work of Michelangelo. The great Renaissance sculptor once said something to the effect that he looked at a block of marble and chiseled away everything that wasn't *David*. ("The more the marble wastes, the more the statue grows" is the remark officially attributed to him in Bartlett's *Familiar Quotations*.) Time and the elements have done something like this for Delicate Arch. One day, Delicate Arch will keel over, but that day is probably far off. Landscape Arch surely will collapse first, and maybe in our lifetime. For all I know, Landscape Arch could topple by the time I finish writing this sentence.

I rounded out the afternoon at Turret Arch, with the sunset light flushing out the North and South windows. Water, ice, extreme temperatures, and the shifting movement of underground salt deposits all played a hand in the creation of these arches. To put it in purely geological terms, things fall apart; the center cannot hold.

MOAB WAS BOTH the son of Lot and the name of an ancient desert kingdom southeast of the Dead Sea. Lot, as we know from reading the Bible, was warned by a pair of angels to flee the city of Sodom, and when his wife looked back to enjoy a glimpse of the destruction, God, in his infinite mercy, turned her into a block of salt. Served her right, too. Naturally, some Mormons had to go and name a town in Utah after all this hilarity. Of course they couldn't call it Sodom, so they used the next-best name. Every summer, tens of thousands of Lycra-clad mountain bikers, hikers, canyoneers, four-wheel-drive enthusiasts in Jeep Wranglers, white-water rafters, foreign backpackers, and the Lonely Planet crowd descend on Moab, the largest town in southeastern Utah, which is to say it is a very small town indeed. All I was looking for was a green-chile cheeseburger. I confess I like Moab. The town is a guilty pleasure. I took a walk down Main Street. The twilight was cooling down and the sky was deep and winy. I strolled past Poison Spider Bicycles, the Moab Climbing Shop, Brig's Moab Outdoors, Summit Canyon Mountaineering, Action Shots (they videotape you shooting the white-water rapids), and the Red River Canoe Company, which offered a choice of paddle trips on Stillwater and Labyrinth canyons, the Colorado, or the Goosenecks of the San Juan. Century 21 wanted to sell me panoramic views of the La Sal Mountains; Canyonlands Realty wanted to put me into a two-story adobe with breathtaking views of Red Canyon. A gallery called the Hogan Trading Company peddled authentic Navajo throw rugs, Hopi kachinas, and Zuni jewelry. The Original Red Dirt Shirt Company sold something called "dirt shirts," hand-dyed by a process utilizing the unadulterated red dirt of Utah's Entrada sandstone. ("This red dirt, which is famous for its long-lasting properties, has been blessed and is believed to bring good luck to the wearer.") Actually the rust-colored T-shirts looked kind of cool. I would have bought one, except I don't believe that a T-shirt should cost more than a fine dinner for two in San Francisco. I had my choice of scarfing down green-chile cheeseburgers at any number of places, including the Slick Rock Cafe, Smitty's Golden Steaks, or Eddie McStiff's Restaurant & Microbrewery. There was an Italian restaurant on Main, Pasta Jay's, and it was packed, but I figured really good Italian cuisine will come to Moab about the same time Naples gets Navajo fry bread.

After dinner, I stopped into Back of Beyond Books, one of the best bookstores in the United States. I bought a copy of the hard-to-find *If Mountains Die: A New Mexico Memoir* by John Nichols, reissued a few years ago by W. W. Norton as a handsome paperback. Pretty much everything Edward Abbey ever wrote, or had written about him, was up there on the bookshelves. There were good maps, guidebooks, environmental titles, and an above-average selection of literary fiction and poetry. I spent about an hour browsing in the bookshop, and then I found myself a cheap motel.

So far, my road trip into the desert Southwest had been like coming into contact with my own vital organs. My time out here had been a restorative, a communication with wilderness and a world that was bringing me to levels of awareness and connections necessary to my well-being. But right now, more than anything else, what I needed was cable TV and a break from the hard ground.

11

A WALK IN THE DESERT

NORTH AND SOUTH Six-shooter Peaks aimed their barrels at the blue Utah sky. It was a flawless morning and I was on my way to the Needles District of Canyonlands National Park. On the road south of Moab, the one leading out to Needles, I stopped by Newspaper Rock to read the latest news, some of it only three thousand years old. For thousands of years, Indians (and others) had been noting their passage by pecking at the dark desert varnish on the rock. Abstract designs, tracings of hands and footprints, squiggle lines, and sacred doodlings, images of deer and bighorn sheep, combined with anthromorphs and hunters on horseback shown shooting their quarry in the buttocks. White pioneers and explorers had added their own graffiti to the rock, marking their passage by the dates. Both the Fremont and Anasazi cultures had been here. The horse drawings were obviously Navajo. (All horse images post-dated the sixteenth century, for it was the Spaniards who brought horses over to the New World.)

I looked hard at the squiggles and bighorn rams, searching for a Kokopelli. Both the Fremont and Anasazi cultures had comingled in this canyon, and their artwork overlapped. While each culture achieved a distinctive artistic style, there may have been some borrowing of technique. The Fremont favored strong geometrical designs for their anthromorphs; the Anasazi style favored the more spidery, ghostly images. In all three sections of Canyonlands, you could find rock art depicting hunting scenes, crop harvesting, abstract designs, shield figures, and stylized masks and faces.

Up Salt Creek Canyon in the Needles District, in a rather difficult reach of the canyon, is a famous Fremont pictograph called All-American Man. Its circular torso is painted with a design of blue and white with red stripes, which makes it look for all the world like an American flag. Of course, there was no official "America" at the time it was painted. And there wouldn't be one for a long time.

There is older artwork, too. Archaic hunter-gatherers predated the Fremont and Anasazi, and they painted pictographs in dark red pigments on the rock panels—the most ghostly and mysterious of all the figures. The Great Gallery in Horseshoe Canyon, far to the west of the Green River, the largest Indian gallery in North America, has a 175-foot panel of rock art showing a row of elongated figures painted in dark red pigments. These human figures, larger than life-size, seem to loom above the canyon bottom. They have no arms, no legs, and faceless skull-shaped heads add to their ghostly effect. These pictographs predate the Fremont and Anasazi, but no one is certain exactly how old they are—some archaeologists say two thousand years old, while others say as many as five thousand. There is a tributary to Horse Canyon, near the Maze, not shown on the maps, that hikers call Pictograph Fork, where visionary figures painted by Archaic hunter-gatherers depict ceremonial harvest scenes that seem to be merging the natural world with the spiritual plane.

As far back as ten thousand years ago, bands of prehistoric hunters roamed the plateau country in search of large game, and their stone spear points have been found throughout Canyonlands. As the giant bison, elk, and other large prey became extinct, these Paleo-Indians evolved into a modified huntergatherer culture that archaeologists refer to as the Archaic. This culture changed, too, around 1000 B.C., with the discovery of agriculture, when the Indians began growing maize. The Archaic nomads grew dependent on their maize and became more sedentary. They started to build stone dwellings and granaries and establish permanent sites. The Archaic culture was giving way to the Fremont culture. The Fremont would later be joined by the Anasazi, who migrated from Mesa Verde in the highlands of southwestern Colorado. Today we look upon their artwork and religious imaging and try to imagine what life must have been like for them on the Colorado Plateau.

It is funny how we allow an artificial complexity to overwhelm our lives. The average reader of the *New York Times* probably gets confronted in a single issue of that newspaper with more information than an Anasazi could ever absorb in a lifetime. And yet the Anasazi probably made more sense out of his world than the *Times* reader makes out of his.

It is one thing to see these images in a photograph or roped off behind a museum display and quite another to encounter them on the wall of a canyon. I can't say which gripped me more, the thought of these people carving their fetishes and symbols on the rocks or the fact that these artworks were still here for us to witness undisturbed. These rock images are not mere artifacts; they are still charged with power, still capable of casting a spell.

I left Newspaper Rock and headed into the Needles District, stopping for a look at Wooden Shoe Arch. I then drove through Squaw Flat to where the pavement ends at the very brink of

Big Spring Canyon Overlook. It would be a 5.1-mile hike from trailhead to trail's end to reach the Confluence Overlook. I wanted to see the Green and Colorado rivers merging together. I shouldered my backpack and began the hike down into the canyon. The cottonwoods below were leafing out in late-spring greenery. I followed the winding trail among boulders, stepping from ledge to ledge. I would have to traverse several canyons in order to get to the confluence. The way was well marked—by footprints on the sandy path and, where the path and sand ran out, by cairns, tiny rock markers, set on the bare stone face of the slickrock.

I crossed the bottom of the first canyon and topped out at the rim beyond. I had a splendid view of mesas and plateaus and the snow-capped La Sals fifty miles to the east. Ahead of me were more canyons of orange-and-white Cedar Mesa sandstone.

The sun was shining, the desert was bright, and I felt great. I had the trail to myself; there were no other hikers around. What a splendid, remote park. If only every other national park could be like this. When I reached a high point on a stony ridge, my second canyon, I was treated to an unobstructed view in all directions. I could see three separate mountain ranges—the La Sals, Abajos, and Henrys. On my left were the incredible sandstone spires known as the Needles, a line of orange-and-pink towers and minarets three hundred feet high. The banded rocks seemed to lean together, as if for moral support.

Close by, growing out of cracks in the rocks, were clumps of fiery Indian paintbrush. It had been a great spring for wildflowers. I was seeing orange globe mallows, yellow daisies, pink four-o'clocks, red skyrocket gilias and hummingbird's trumpets, blue larkspurs and lupines, and the well-named Indian paintbrush, which does indeed resemble an artist's delicate brush point dipped in scarlet paint. Most prominent were the displays of prickly pear cacti. These cactus flowers were either a flame saffron or a wine-colored violet. I even spied the far less abundant brilliant red cactus that is called a claret cup.

On the ground was cryptogamic soil—dry, crunchy, alive. Here was the first step in the transformation of bare sand into organic soil. Bright green shrubs known as single-leaf ash grew in the canyon bottoms. Twisted evergreen junipers, their trunks weathered a silvery gray, took root in cracks in the rocks. The Needles seemed to be changing color by the hour.

I took another healthy hit from my canteen. The sun was fierce. I tugged at the back of my shirt; sweat was making it stick. It had that salty stiffness clothing gets when you sweat and then dry off and then sweat again.

I descended from the high rock canyons into the first of the grabens, a narrow parallel sink in the ground called Devils Lane, bordered by steep rocky walls. The graben was hot and dry and rather dull compared to the wonderful slickrock canyons I had been traversing. The foot path intersected with an old Jeep trail, and when a Jeep Wrangler passed me, filled with people, my reverie was broken. After hours of hiking, I couldn't help but feel that those folks in the Jeep were cheating just a little.

I came out upon the Confluence Overlook. The Colorado and Green rivers met and merged fifteen hundred feet beneath the talus slope. The muddy Colorado came in from a deep canyon on the right, the golden Green on the left. The Colorado was a dull brown with vegetable green tints; the Green was a muddier yellow. They flowed side by side, and would remain so for about a mile, before becoming indistinguishable. The division between the two was marked by distinct colors and lines of driftwood. The Green and Colorado were still running a little high from the spring runoff. A few miles downriver, unseen from the Confluence Overlook, at a place called Spanish Bottom, the Colorado would round a bend and hit the first of twenty-six rapids in Cataract Canyon. A nice little surprise for John Wesley Powell and his crew. In Powell's time, the confluence was considered the beginning of the Colorado River (named after its reddish color, not for the Rocky Mountain state) and the river upstream of the Colorado was called the Grand. At Cataract Canyon, huge blocks of rock fell from overhead with some regularity, crashing into the river, creating great jagged barriers in the streambed. The passing water was ripped into boiling standing waves, some as high and big around as a four-story building. Among the twenty-six rapids in Cataract Canyon are three truly killer drops. I saw below me four brightly colored rafts bound for Spanish Bottom. Today people pay good money to do what rightly scared the hell out of John Wesley Powell and his crew. I tried to imagine the sound and reverberation from the approaching rapids—probably something like the BART train running underneath the pavement of Market Street in San Francisco.

Up here on the overlook, the river couldn't be heard at all. It slid silently and serenely around the bend, its colors not yet mixing, but flowing side by side. I looked out over the far rim; out there was the Land of Standing Rocks, the beginnings of the Maze. Junction Butte and Grandview Point rose up from behind the confluence, the tip of the high mesa known as Island in the Sky. I dug the scene, enjoying my lunch of raisins and peanuts, and then began the hike back.

I CAMPED THAT evening at Needles Outpost, just outside the national park. There was no groundwater; water had to be hauled into camp. It was an excellent campground, almost primitive, with spectacular views of the Needles and Bagpipe Butte.

The desert at twilight was as mysterious as I've ever seen it.

Jackrabbits ran about in the sagebrush. The sunset shined behind billowing clouds. I climbed a high red sandstone butte behind my campsite. The view from up here was extraordinary. A few of the other campers joined me on this high yet comfortable perch to watch the sunset.

A little blond boy, about four years old, came out of his family's camper in search of his daddy. He scampered up the red rock in his bare feet to join him. It was really a very easy climb for the boy and pefectly safe. His little legs took him high above the scene. He was totally unafraid, a self-confident little boy. I wondered what the boy would remember of this evening, if anything. He was of that age where one is not so much aware of things as a part of them. There was no "self" to separate him from the desert evening. No endings or beginnings for the boy, just a world pouring into him and through him. If he remembered anything at all of this day, perhaps his memories would come back to him on a rush of light.

The spires of the Needles fired up bright orange in the sundown. The sun sank away and the sky deepened from a royal blue to a dark purple-violet. The Needles and Bagpipe Butte were outlined in a final alpenglow. The moment felt timeless.

12

INDIAN COUNTRY

I WAS LISTENING to the news on the car radio. The largest manhunt in the history of southeastern Utah was under way all around me. The entire town of Bluff had been evacuated. A few days back, three fugitives dressed in camouflage had murdered a police officer just over the state line in Cortez, Colorado, and now they were on the run and shooting at anything that moved. It was like being in a Sam Peckinpah movie.

The three fugitives were being described as "survivalists." Some vague political motive was said to be behind their crime spree. For as yet obscure reasons, these three idiots had hijacked a large water truck near Cortez. Water trucks are built a little like armored cars; it was thought the desperadoes perhaps intended to crash one into the side of a bank and rob it. A local patrolman, Dale Claxton, spotted the stolen vehicle and pulled them over. As he was waiting in his car for backup, the men in the water truck opened fire on him with automatic weapons, killing him. A wild chase ensued. Two deputy sheriffs, Jason Bishop and Todd Martin, were shot and wounded by the getaway men. The gunmen ditched the water truck and commandeered a flatbed pickup, escaping down the McElmo Canyon Road. A short time later, Art Hutchinson, the superintendent of Hovenweep National Monument, just over the border in Utah, was driving along a road outside the park when his vehicle was suddenly sprayed by gunfire. He escaped injury. The flatbed pickup truck was later found abandoned, along with two automatic rifles, in rugged Cross Canyon near the Utah-Colorado border.

By this time, hundreds of trackers and cops were swarming over the area, trying to find these guys. Blackhawk helicopters flew armed searchers into the labyrinth of canyons. The Dolores River (River of Sorrows) was closed to boaters. Roadblocks went up and tracks matching those of two of the suspects were identified near Cross Canyon. But the trackers could find no further clues and the trail grew cold.

Investigators released the names and mug shots: Jason McVean and Robert Matthew Mason, both twenty-six, and both from Durango, and Alan "Monte" Pilon, thirty, who made his home in the tiny Colorado community of Dove Creek. All three were said to be fascinated by automatic weaponry and had a reputation as backcountry survivalists. It was not immediately clear whether they were affiliated with any antigovernment militias, although it would be later reported they had been thrown out of a militia for being too violent and scary.

By now two hundred officers from thirty-four law-enforcement agencies in four states were swarming over the area. They discovered an abandoned Ford truck and a camper belonging to the suspects parked alongside each other at the Animas River Park in Durango. A search revealed camping gear, food, and five homemade pipe bombs. McVean's empty flatbed Nissan truck was discovered on Cherry Creek Road near Mancos. Two bunkers containing caches of food were found near Bug Point, southwest of Dove Creek.

Americans have a love affair with the Wild West but prefer to have their bad guys played by Paul Newman and Robert Redford. When real sociopaths start shooting, attitudes change. A state social worker was enjoying his lunch near the San Juan River just outside the town of Bluff, Utah, when a man dressed in camouflage fired a shot at him and missed. A Utah lawman, San Juan County Deputy Sheriff Kelly Bradford, arriving on the scene, was shot in the back by a sniper who used a .308 high-caliber rifle from a distance of three hundred yards. Luckily, Deputy Sheriff Bradford survived this assassination attempt. A short time later, the police uncovered the body of suspect Robert Mason nearby, dead by his own hand, killed with the rifle he had used to shoot the deputy. A handgun was found near the body, along with three pipe bombs.

The entire town of Bluff was evacuated as the search intensified along the brush-covered banks of the San Juan River. Two hundred National Guardsmen arrived for the manhunt. Now, I live in San Francisco, where on any given day there might be a dozen armed fugitive murderers walking around, and no one gives it a second thought—but this was something else. The citizens of Bluff really had genuine cause to be terrified.

The searchers beat the bushes but found nothing. They even set fire to the overgrown brush and willows along the San Juan's banks, hoping to smoke them out. Police began to suspect that the two fugitives had doubled back and might be in hiding in the original search area around Cross Canyon. Bluff's residents finally were allowed back into their town.

Hovenweep National Monument was closed to tourists and campers for a second time. Rafting was banned on the San Juan. The Grand Gulch Primitive Area was placed off-limits. I had been looking forward to backpacking in Grand Gulch. Grand Gulch isn't a gulch, but a magnificent wild canyon of blond sandstone walls and green cottonwoods. There are miles of side canyons with pueblo ruins, petroglyph etchings and pictographs. In cliff niches stand stone storehouses, ruins built on ledges, and handprints of long-dead Anasazi pressed into the rock face. They say you can feel the invisible eyes of the Anasazi watching you as you hike down in the canyon. Now you might be feeling the eyes of Jason McVean and Alan Pilon.

As I passed through the town of Blanding, radio reports were informing listeners that searchers were combing the rugged outback in the vicinity of Natural Bridges National Monument. A special emphasis was being placed on the Grand Gulch Primitive Area to the south. That's where I was headed—Natural Bridges National Monument. I would have concentrated the search north of the monument, near the old Hidden Splendor Mine. That was the spot I would choose to hide, but purely for literary reasons. The Hidden Splendor, an abandoned uranium mine, was where Doc, Bonnie, Seldom Seen, and Hayduke hid out when they were on the lam in *The Monkey Wrench Gang*. What a vantage point our maniacs would have. They would be able to see everything from their perch atop the Hidden Splendor. They would have an unobstructed view of the white sandstones of Natural Bridges and Cedar Mesa shining a thousand feet below and five miles south of them. There would be the dim outline of Navajo Mountain, near the Arizona border, and the great volcanic plug of Shiprock rising up in New Mexico. With their binoculars, they could sweep the Kaiparowitz Plateau and the Waterpocket Fold, the deep gorge of the Dirty Devil River, the dark Henrys joggling the horizon, and the pink sandstone of Glen Canyon. They could see anyone coming for miles.

Unfortunately on this day, Natural Bridges National Monument was the safest place in southeastern Utah. There weren't enough bullets in the bandoliers of the desperadoes to take out even half the tourists swarming over the parking lots high above the three stone bridges. Where were terrorists when you needed them?

The second- and third-largest natural stone bridges in the world are to be found here in the monument. The largest stone bridge in the world, Rainbow Bridge, is over in Glen Canyon, near the Arizona border. There is a distinction to be made between bridges and arches. Natural bridges are carved by stream erosion; arches are dry spans with no streams running beneath them. Arches stand against the skyline; bridges form in the bottoms of deep canyons. Both arches and bridges begin as narrow fins of sandstone, with water the dissolving agent—seeping moisture and frost in the case of arches, and running water in the case of bridges. The water dissolves the cement between the grains of sand and then frost wedging and gravity take over.

Owachomo Bridge, the oldest of the three stone spans in the monument, and the most graceful and delicate, worn flat and thin by time, no longer has a stream flowing beneath it. Frost action and seeping moisture continue to shape it. It could crack fatally at any given time, or stand for centuries.

Kachina Bridge, the youngest of the spans, looms large and bulky above White Canyon. A sluggish stream inches beneath the blond rock. I could detect a green muck smell down there in the willows and cottonwoods at the canyon bottom. It was hard to believe that this creek was still carving away the sandstone. But thunderstorms brought on flash floods that still worked to enlarge the span.

The largest bridge, Sipapu, is difficult to spot from the rim of the canyon. Its abutments stand far from the creek, so it has endured little stream erosion, except in exceptionally high floods. Of the three bridges, Sipapu has the highest and greatest span. It is the second-largest natural stone bridge in the world.

Clarence Dutton, the nineteenth-century geologist, explored

the canyon. In 1904, *National Geographic* publicized the bridges. Teddy Roosevelt declared Natural Bridges a national monument in 1908—Utah's first. A year later, President Taft expanded the boundaries to protect nearby pueblo ruins, and the General Land Office assigned the bridges their current Hopi Indian names. Their first official names, I am sorry to report, were President, Senator, and Congressman, in order of height. A little later on, some explorers renamed them Augusta, Caroline, and Edwina, after relatives, a slight improvement. The Navajo, who lived in the area, had no known name for the bridges; neither did the Paiute, who called the canyon Ma-Vah-Talk-Tump, meaning "under the horse's belly."

The Hopi names were chosen because explorers noticed that the pueblo ruins found near the bridges were in many ways identical to cliff dwellings occupied by the Hopi in Arizona. When they spoke to the Hopi, this was made clear. The Hopi were, in fact, the direct descendants of the ancient Pueblo culture known as the Anasazi, who had inhabited so much of the Southwest. The Hopi, for the past four hundred years, have been living on or near three large finger mesas overlooking the Painted Desert in northern Arizona. Places like Natural Bridges National Monument are still stops along the sacred migration paths of a number of Hopi clans. The Hopi are able to identify Anasazi paintings on the canyon walls as their own clan symbols. To this day, Hopi elders annually visit these sites and shrines throughout the Southwest, places that include Natural Bridges National Monument, leaving ritual offerings of prayer feathers and small bundles of plants. Take a moment and think about this uninterrupted link to the past. The Hopi religion—which is basically the religion of the Anasazi—might predate the Judeo-Christian tradition.

The name Owachomo means "rock mound," named after a

large rounded rock mass found on the bridge's northeastern buttress. Rock art on the second bridge bears a resemblance to symbols found on Hopi kachina dolls, thus the name Kachina, or "spirit dancer." Sipapu, the name given to the largest bridge, means "the place of emergence"—literally, the earth's vagina. The Sipapu was the opening through which humanity emerged into the world.

And speaking of humanity, I needed to get away from it. I had been spoiled by the emptiness of the Escalante and the remoteness of Canyonlands. Time to do some walking and check out those bridges from the bottom of the canyon. Perhaps there would be fewer tourists there. That is to say, fewer people exactly like myself. But I was wrong. The footpaths were just as crowded and the canyon bottoms jammed with my fellow human beings.

I TOOK THE monument turnoff road to the junction of Utah 95 and then turned right onto 261, heading south over the juniper-covered mesa. I drove straight for thirty miles, until suddenly, and with little warning, the world fell away.

A sign where the highway abruptly ended warned vehicles to slow down and come to a complete halt. And for good reason. Cedar Mesa ends here, dropping a straight thousand feet to the desert below. I had seen this eleven years before, on my first trip to the Southwest, and it was the most memorable driving experience of my trip. From up here, I had a completely unobstructed view of southern Utah and northern Arizona, one of the most stunning views in the country. Spreading out below me were the orange-red formations known as Valley of the Gods, and in the distance was Monument Valley.

To get there, I had to jounce down an unpaved road called the Moki Dugway, three miles of dangerous hairpins hanging over the side of a cliff, dropping a straight thousand feet to the red desert below. You can bet I drove this as carefully and painstakingly as any road I have ever ridden on.

At the foot of the Moki Dugway, a dirt road headed east into Valley of the Gods, a spectacular sixteen-mile drive through stunning monoliths of red sandstone. But I continued due south toward Monument Valley, which was shimmering in the distance.

The monuments rose up grandly out of a sea of light. Out of these red sand dunes and desert grow little but snakeweed, rabbitbrush, a few stunted junipers, and a scattering of yuccas. Barely enough plant life to add touches of green to the swimming red scenery. At a quick glance, the desert appeared dry and barren. But there were hidden water and wildflowers here and Navajo sheep grazed on what little grass grew.

The sand dunes rolled up into a clear blue sky highlighted by sheer red buttes and colossal brown mesas. The two-lane blacktop was too narrow and winding for its 65 mph posting. This was a dangerous road, and I felt vulnerable even in the heavy Blazer. And yet cars and trucks whizzed by me with little regard for safety. This was to be something I would experience everywhere I drove in Navajo country.

The buttes and monuments grew closer. I was reminded that wind and water had carved everything before my eyes. Monument Valley is no valley, but the bed of an ancient sea. A long wearing-down of alternate layers of soft and hard rock reveal the wonders of Monument Valley. Up close, the towering rock formations appear to be a warm chocolate brown in color.

I turned into Monument Valley Navajo Tribal Park. Cheesy curio shops had been set up at the entrance road so that the Navajo could peddle rugs and jewelry to the tourists. I stopped to enjoy an Indian taco at a roadside stand—shredded meat, beans, and chopped lettuce on fry bread, wholesome but very bland. Three dollars and fifty cents bought me a bellyful. The young Navajo girl who served me from her wooden stand seemed very shy. A small dog looked at the treat in my hand but backed away every time I approached to pet him. Two Navajo women in velveteen blouses and satiny ankle-length skirts of vivid blue and green worked at looms in the shade of a ramada, weaving traditional rugs. Local color for the tourist trade—most of the Navajo, men and women, were wearing jeans. Finishing the taco, I drove out to the visitor's center, its pennants flapping wildly in the strong wind.

From the visitor's center, an unpaved loop trail covered seventeen miles of spectacular valley views. Monument Valley is splendid from a distance, but to really appreciate what's out here, you have to see it all up close. You can do this for a small fee by risking your own vehicle on the axle-busting dirt road. Or you can spend a little more money and hire one of the tour vans that work out of the parking lot next to the visitor's center. I decided on the former. I had vowed during my trip to avoid all guided tours. This might have been a mistake, as the Navajo guides had reputations as great wits who were not adverse to pulling the leg of the *belagana*.

The parking lot was a madhouse. The wind was kicking up dust, the pennants made flapping noises, and vehicles moved about in all directions with no semblance of order. I started down the bumpy grade leading to the loop trail and was immediately passed by a heavy-duty army-style Jeep, one of the tour vehicles, crammed with sightseers hanging on for dear life. These six-wheel-drive vehicles can get you through terrain that would have stopped Rommel. They call these "shake 'n' bake" tours. The loop road was like a scene out of *The Road Warrior*.

Dunes and sand flats erupted into solitary buttes and escarpments. Freestanding rock formations rose against a blue sky. On my left appeared the well-known Mittens, their "hands of time" welcoming me to Monument Valley. These twin buttes, with slender opposable thumbs, did indeed appear to resemble a pair of mittens. They were a rich chocolate brown under the afternoon sun. The underlying sandstone on the buttes, de Chelly sandstone, was crowned by a harder rock of the Shinarump Formation. The softer Organ Rock shale found at the base of these cliffs had eroded out into stairlike horizontal terraces, forming sloping foundations. All the monuments were quite shapely and mysterious.

I came upon John Ford's Point, the film director's favorite shooting location. Behind me rose the standing rocks known as the Three Sisters—nuns, not siblings. Two older nuns seemed to be leading a slender novice between them, perhaps on their way to vespers. Ford's Point provided tremendous views of Elephant and Camel buttes, the Thumb, and the North Window. I would have enjoyed Ford's Point, but the area was like a traffic jam in Naples. Complete confusion, with drivers making up their own rules on the spot.

Ford directed six of his Westerns here, including *Stagecoach* and *The Searchers*. Monument Valley was still a well-kept secret back in Ford's day. Around 1938, a great landscape photographer named Josef Muench, who had befriended the Navajo, was doing considerable shooting in this then little-known spot in the northern Arizona desert. His Monument Valley photographs were appearing with regularity in a tourist publication called *Arizona Highways*. Muench was a German immigrant who had fallen in love with the American West; his other claim to fame, besides his photographs, was that he had once thrown a tomato at a young German politician named Adolf Hitler. Muench had a friend named Harry Goulding, who had started up the nearby Goulding's Trading Post just outside of Monument Valley. Goulding was going broke selling groceries to the Navajo. There was much to see in Monument Valley, but few people to see it. Goulding felt the place needed publicity. Through the grapevine, he heard that United Artists in Hollywood was planning to make a Western called *Stagecoach*. So he had Muench prepare a booklet of black-and-white photographs to tempt director John Ford and Walter Wanger, the production chief of United Artists, into shooting their movie on location at Monument Valley. One look at the photographs and Ford and Wanger were sold. At the time, no roads led into Monument Valley; Ford had to construct them to bring in his film crew.

Forgive me, but I am not a fan of John Ford. I don't like his strong westerners, his noble red men, or his phony micks. The West was not won by true grit, rugged individualism, or John Wayne, but by communitarianism and huge federal entitlement programs, such as the Homestead Act, the Mining Act, the Grazing Act, and the Timber Act, railroad subsidies, and taxpayer-financed irrigation projects. John Ford's whitewashing of manifest destiny has about as much credence as Oliver Stone's latter-day theories on the Kennedy assassination.

A tour Jeep thundered past, kicking up a rooster tail of dust. The wind whipped up sand, blowing it all around. Not a single hiking trail in Monument Valley was open to unescorted visitors. You could hire a Navajo guide to take you out there into the red sands and hardpan desert, but otherwise you were confined to the loop trail.

It was also impolite to photograph any Navajo without first asking permission. And you were expected to tip. After all, they were pros. So many movie crews and ad agencies have shot footage in Monument Valley that it is said that even the Navajo horses know where to stand.

The Navajo make up the largest Indian tribe in North America. One out of every seven Native Americans in the United States is a Navajo. Monument Valley is only a small part of their 25,000-square-mile reservation, the largest in the United

States. Navajoland stretched across the horizons of the Four Corners, a high desert and canyon country of wide vistas and unearthly land formations, where Arizona, New Mexico, Utah, and Colorado all converge. The bulk of the Navajo Reservation occupies northeastern Arizona, and juts out into neighboring Utah and New Mexico. The Arizona-Utah state line runs through the middle of Monument Valley. The Indians call their huge reservation the Navajo Nation, although it is a nation surrounded by a larger nation, the United States.

The Navajo are blessed with some of the most eerily beautiful and unspoiled landscape on earth. The Navajo accept their place in the natural order and merge into the landscape, feeling little need to alter or transform it. The Navajo call this *hozho,* "harmony." They inhabit a timeless landscape, full of form and elegance. When Navajo take their leave of one another, they have a departing phrase, *Nih zhonigo,* "Walk in beauty." The scale of their home is vast, the sky above it even vaster and more infinite. The desert seems ancient yet freshly created. When one lives with a sense of place, the world feels secure and filled with promise. The Navajo wear the desert like their skin and walk in harmony, and like a religion, the land shapes the important decisions of their lives.

The Southwest may be a sacred landscape to the Navajo, but it is also a borrowed landscape. The Navajo are relative newcomers; to the Hopi, they are invaders. The Hopi called them "Head-Pounders." Linguists and anthropologists have traced the Navajo to the Athabascan-speaking peoples of northwestern Canada. The Athabascans slowly migrated south from the plains of Canada, probably over the fourteenth and fifteenth centuries, traveling in small, materially poor bands, living mainly by hunting and gathering. Their own legends describe an ancestral journey from world to world. By 1500, they were firmly established in the Southwest. The Spanish invaders would show up just a few decades later. (*Navajo* is a Spanish word; the Navajo call themselves *Dineh*—"the people." They call their desert homeland the *Dinetah*.) Nomadic hunters, at first they had little culture of their own. When not staging raids on the peaceful Hopi and other Pueblo people, they were learning from them and adapting to their ways. From the agrarian Hopi, they got corn and dry farming, pottery making, ceremonial dancing, and, I suspect, a lot of their metaphysical beliefs. But ever the wandering nomads, they preferred to live not in cities built against cliff faces, like the Pueblos, but spread out over the wide-open landscape. Soon after the Spanish arrived, the Navajo became adept horsemen, sheepherders, weavers, and silversmiths. They had a knack for adopting a culture and making it their own. Just look at their pickup trucks, jeans, and cowboy hats.

All cultures evolve creation myths to justify their national origins. The polite fiction of the First Thanksgiving mythologizes the founding of our country by Englishmen. Modern America has Hollywood and John Ford to explain our dreams of westward expansion. In Navajo tradition, there were underworlds before the earth was formed, each existing on different levels. When the Dineh emerged from the Dark Underworld, into the Red Underworld, everything they saw was red and barren. This could be a description of a place not unlike the Colorado Plateau. To the Navajo, the Southwest was the sacred center of the earth. First Man and First Woman formed the earth. Changing Woman created human beings from her dwelling place on Fir Mountain, one of the inner mountains in the Navajo landscape. Spider Woman, from her perch atop Spider Rock in Canyon de Chelly, gave birth to the gods of earth and sky, moon, sun, and stars, and all the plants, animals, humans, and the rain. And so on. In Navajo mythology, so far as I know, no dim ancestral image survives of the dark spruce forests of Canada.

I rounded the bend between Raingod and Thunderbird mesas, my Blazer managing to find every crater in the road. I had a good view of Totem Pole, a needle-thin spire, and the rocky splinters known as the Yeibichai. Many visitors to Monument Valley complain that the Navajo deliberately left their loop road in this awful condition in order to gull tourists into taking their paid tours. But I approved of the primitive roadway. The more chuckholes the better.

I would have liked to have gone out and looked at the Navajo horse drawings on the rocks, but that would have required a guide. The Anasazi once lived in Monument Valley, and their petroglyphs and pictographs have survived on the rocks here. There are small ruins out there, but none of the large Anasazi dwellings one finds south of Monument Valley near Kayenta. The rock formations in Monument Valley did not produce the kind of large overhangs and caves favored by the Anasazi.

I also would have liked to have left the madness of the loop road in order to enjoy some of the peace and stillness of Monument Valley. All that sky and empty space. Out there, a human being is only an expression of nature, and landscape a display of something deeper. The word *religion* doesn't even begin to do justice to what lies out there, because the word creates a needless disconnection. Call it the great mystery, if you need to call it anything. In the Navajo tongue, there is no word for *religion*.

I MADE IT out to Tsegi Canyon in Navajo National Monument two hours before sunset. There was a great little campground hidden in the junipers where one could tent for free. The campground provided water and nothing else. Although I had arrived late, there were still plenty of empty campsites. Not many people take the trouble to come out here. Navajo National Monument is a little off the beaten path. The monument protects three fabulous Anasazi ruins. It was named after the Navajo because they were the last inhabitants of the region. It was they who had discovered and named the ruins. The word *Anasazi* is itself a Navajo term. This word has been variously mistranslated as "ancient ones" or "old ones" or "those who were here before us." But the more precise translation is "enemy ancestors." The Navajo realized that these early inhabitants of the desert Southwest, the ones who had left behind their art images and stone ruins among the cliffs, were the ancient ancestors of their enemies, the Hopi. The Anasazi, who encompassed different desert people, were the antecedents of all modern Pueblo people, Hopi, Acoma, Tewa, Zuni, and the others.

I pitched a tent and followed a footpath called the Sandal Trail to the rim of a narrow canyon filled with Douglas fir and rustling green aspens. It was high and cool up on the rim of Tsegi Canyon, well over seven thousand feet above sea level. On the other side of the canyon, far below, was the ancient village of Betatakin, set down into a huge alcove in the canyon wall. I mean *huge*. The cave is five hundred feet above the canyon floor and houses about 135 connected stone dwellings. I needed binoculars to pick out details of the rock city far below me. The overlook gave me a spectacular cross-canyon view.

Three stone-wall dwellings had been set into the bedrock ledges. These contained clusters of masonry rooms. In Navajo, *betatakin* means "ledge house." The Hopi called this place Kawestima and they called their ancestors the Hisatsinom, not the Anasazi. Perhaps it's better we use the Navajo terms today. If Navajo is tough for white people to pronounce, Hopi is the ultimate tongue twister.

The great alcove in the canyon wall was deep enough to provide shelter for the ancient ones, and because it faced south, it was warmed by the winter sun. The Anasazi grew their crops in fields located a mile down the canyon. But it also looked like a very precarious dwelling place. I wondered how the Anasazi kept their children from falling off the ledges to their deaths. There is a theory that the Anasazi lived in these dangerous aeries as a defensive gesture against maurauding enemies. The ruins here all line up in geometric patterns, which suggests to anthropologists that the Anasazi could warn one another with signals when attackers were coming.

Ancient Pueblo cultures varied throughout the Southwest. Archaeologists have divided these regional cultures into three branches, based on pottery styles and architecture: those living in Chaco Canyon, in what is now New Mexico; those who dwelt atop Mesa Verde, in what is now southwestern Colorado; and the Anasazi here in Kayenta. The Kayenta people developed distinctive pottery styles that are easily recognizable to the experienced eye.

The Anasazi were themselves the descendants of Paleo-Indians who migrated to the Southwest. By 5500 B.C., the Anasazi were in their hunter-gatherer phase. Their earliest period of settlement—known as the Basket Maker phase—began sometime after the birth of Christ and lasted about seven hundred years. During this period, the Anasazi were found dispersed around the mesa tops, living in permanent pit-house dwellings. These windowless designs provided protection from the elements and not much else. The Anasazi entered their dwellings through roof openings directly over the fire pits—and this must have been the source of a few entertaining accidents.

The Pueblo phase of the Anasazi began around A.D. 750 and lasted until around 1300. They built aboveground stone and masonry dwellings that could house several hundred people,

like the ones here in Tsegi Canyon. During this period, the Anasazi developed subsurface round rooms, or kivas, which were
used for both ceremonial and other, more basic, purposes.
Around this time, they also developed practical methods of irrigation. They stored surplus crops in storage chambers with
grooved doorjambs inside their dwellings and in granaries high
up in the canyon walls.

The Anasazi occupied the pueblos of Tsegi Canyon only
briefly, for a mere five decades in the final half of the thirteenth
century, before abandoning their stone cities, possibly due to
drought and crop failure, or perhaps because of internal and
political dissension. Possibly, invading enemies overcame their
defenses. What a loss Betatakin and Keet Seel must have been
to them. So much work and splendor gone. And what a fine
canyon they walked away from.

The rangers did not permit unescorted trips down into Tsegi
Canyon. They didn't want anyone ripping off artifacts or otherwise damaging the ruins. One could arrange to take ranger-
led trips to Betatakin and Keet Seel, the largest Pueblo ruin in
Tsegi Canyon. Betatakin was a five-mile round-trip, and Keet
Seel a steep eight-mile hike, one way, into the canyon, a trip
best done as an overnight backpacking tour. Another ruin, the
small and fragile Inscription House, had been closed to the public for almost thirty years. I thought seriously about the group
trip to Betatakin but was wedded to my no-tour rule.

In camp that evening, I was approached by my neighbor,
who was parked nearby in a very odd-looking, oddly shaped
RV vehicle with—of all things—Dutch license plates.

"*Lonely Planet*," he said. He was referring to the guidebook I
was reading while sitting at my picnic table. I was leafing through
the book, preparing my next day's drive to the Hopi mesas.

"I noticed your van," I said. "You're from Holland?"

"My wife and I have just retired," he told me. His remark

surprised me—he was no older than I was, in his mid-forties. Apparently, he and his wife were taking advantage of their country's famous cradle-to-grave socialism. Naturally, his English was flawless. As I've said before, only Americans are proud of being monolingual.

"We gave up our home and put everything into our RV," the Dutchman said. "We're on a world tour." He had shipped the van over to the United States. "We've been to New York City, Niagara Falls, British Columbia, and Alaska. We left San Francisco last month and we have been seeing the desert."

He explained that they were "bush camping"—just pulling their vehicle over to the side of a road and driving as far into the rough as their wheels would take them. Which was pretty hard without four-wheel drive, but they were managing.

"You can't do this in Europe," he said. "They'll arrest you in your camper if you park alongside a road." He and his wife were making it a habit of staying at free campgrounds such as this one in Navajo National Monument.

"We want to stay here longer," he said, "but we lost our visa and can't get it renewed. So we're going to Mexico. We're going to drive down to Peru."

"On the Pan American Highway?" I was shocked. It was only the most dangerous road in the western hemisphere.

"We're not worried," he said. "No one down there is at war right now."

But there were still plenty of bandits. And worse, police. I suggested he might want to bring along plenty of cash to grease the palms of cops and border guards. Banditos south of the border; armed survivalists up here shooting up the landscape as if in a bad Western. Nothing changes. The Dutchman asked me what he should see between here and Mexico, and I recommended the Grand Canyon's North Rim. I envied him and his wife and wished them well on their adventure of a lifetime.

13

BREATH SPIRITS

WE AMERICANS ARE under the impression that ours is a young country, when, in fact, ours is an ancient land. Our ignorance would be a tragedy if it weren't so damn funny. We have been taught as schoolchildren that the first American towns were established in the Virginia and Massachusetts colonies in the 1600s. And because we believe this to be true, Americans do not have a true history. To paraphrase Santayana, those who cannot remember the past are doomed to repeat the seventh grade.

The Hopi know how old America is. Old Oraibi, perched on the edge of Third Mesa, overlooking the Painted Desert in Arizona, is one of the oldest continuously inhabited villages in the United States. It is almost as old as medieval Dublin. The village of Old Oraibi was established sometime around A.D. 1150 by wandering bands of Anasazi, and these Americans have been living uninterrupted in these same stone dwellings for the past 850 years.

I drove southwest past the tableland known as Black Mesa, sacred to both the Navajo and Hopi. At Tuba City, I turned east onto what is the oldest thoroughfare in North America. A foot trace, it once led from the Hopi mesas all the way to the New Mexican pueblos; this trace is now Arizona Highway 264. The road followed a valley between the southern rim of Black Mesa and the jutting finger mesas of the Hopi reservation. A wind-blown dust shifted all around. This mesa country was austere, almost bleak, the Hopi buttes' dark basaltic formations rising above the buff emptiness of the Painted Desert. Down below the cliffs, close by the road, in bowl-shaped hollows, grew the small patch farms and gardens of the Hopi. Like their ancestral Anasazi, the Hopi are experts at dry farming, growing corn, squash, and melons, and relying not on irrigation but on cere-mony and prayer to bring in a scant annual rainfall. Looking toward the southwest, I could see the San Francisco Peaks, "sa-cred breathing mountains," revered by the Hopi. The moun-tains did indeed appear to breathe. Oscillating air and vapor were trapped by the peaks, and this brought rain to the parched desert. Coronado, in his account of his plunders of the South-west, complained of the dry desert and the lack of abundant food for his men and horses. Yet the Pueblo people managed to coax a satisfactory subsistence from this land.

A winding dirt road led from the highway up to the vaguely medieval-looking village of Old Oraibi on Third Mesa. I parked up front by one of the craft shops so as not to kick up dust. The village, built out of rocks taken from the mesa, blended perfectly with the color and forms of the desert it overlooked. The drab landscape, with its ancient stone architecture, resem-bled a classic Pueblo scene. But there was a disconnect to the place. Next to ancient stone walls and snug mortar and chink dwellings were modern concrete-block houses, parked auto-mobiles, TV antennas, and clotheslines hung with laundry flap-ping in the breeze. This was no historic ruin; this was a town

where people actually lived. What at first appeared as a cluster
of abandoned stone relics was actually a living community.

Old Oraibi is a classic Pueblo town, with stone houses,
ground-level doorways, and dirt paths and walkways. Modern
four-by-four framed windows had been installed in a few of
the older structures. Ladders lead up to flat rooftops, even on
the modern concrete houses. Although I saw modern cinder-
block homes built alongside the ancient stone dwellings, I did
not see a single sloped or peaked roof. The Hopi homes were
carefully oriented toward the sun. The oldest houses had thick
walls, fashioned out of stones and mud mortar that had been
dug out of the local soil. These stone dwellings soak up and
store the warm sunshine and protect the Hopi from the cold
northwest winds.

I spotted a ladder emerging from a kiva, a subterranean ceremonial chamber. I knew enough not to enter or mess around
the kiva. None but those initiated into the clan can be admitted
inside one. I knew from my reading that down inside the kiva
would be stone benches alongside the walls, a fireplace and a
draft-reflecting stone, and, most important, for theological purposes, a notch or crease in the floor known as a *sipapu*. The
Hopi speak of former levels of existence, and of their emergence
into this world, the fourth and final level of existence. The Australian novelist Thomas Keneally visited the Hopi mesas and
he used the *sipapu* as the central metaphor for a book he wrote
about the experience, *The Place Where Souls Are Born*. "This is
the place of emergence," Keneally wrote, "the notch through
which souls enter the visible universe, climbing out of a moth-
ering earth by way of the kiva's ladder and so entering the
surface life of the world. Life came through the sipapu, the
earth's vagina, the place where souls are born. All the energy
and ambiguity of mankind climbs up that ladder."

From up on the mesa, the view of the dull buff-colored desert was stark and beautiful and even a little bleak. Sheer cliffs dropped on three sides to the desert floor. It put me in mind of the novelist Thomas McGuane's wonderful phrase about how we all enjoy abyss frontage. The wind was so strong, I felt it might blow me over the edge of the mesa.

I walked to a house containing a tiny shop in the back where tourist information could be obtained. Tourists are welcome at most Hopi villages but are asked to observe certain protocols. The primary one is to stay out of those underground chambers with ladders coming out of the hatchways—the kivas. Tourists are asked not to photograph any of the Hopi without first obtaining permission; a gratuity is expected. Hopi are available for free guided tours, but, again, a gratuity is expected. Visitors are expected to stay out of the Hopi homes unless invited inside. And don't hold your breath waiting for that to happen. Once for a short period in the seventies, the elders closed off Old Oraibi to all non-Indian visitors, so frustrated were they over the rudeness of tourists who kept barging uninvited into Hopi homes.

Never had I seen a potential tourist trap so little concerned with tourism. In the first place, there is little room up on the mesas for the infrastructure needed to handle tourism—bathrooms, food and water, shelter, and emergency services. Which is just fine with the Hopi. Only this one small shop in Old Oraibi posted information for visitors. Inside, I examined a small collection of pottery and kachina dolls and purchased a fascinating monograph on the Hopi written by John Wesley Powell. Powell, an amateur Indian ethnologist as well as a geologist, had made a study of the Hopi villages, the ancient province of Tusayan, on a later trip he made to the Grand Canyon country.

I was a little disappointed that I had not arrived for one of the many ceremonial dances held on the mesas. Starting a month before the winter solstice, from November through July, at times prescribed by the sun priests, men in several religious societies don elaborate and beautifully painted kachina masks and dance in the village plazas.

A few kachina dances are open to the public; many more are closed. It is left up to the dozen or so individual villages on the Hopi mesas to determine whether the ceremonies will be open to non-Indian visitors. There is great concern that the religious nature of the dances might be trivialized by turning them into tourist spectacles. There is also the practical matter of there being simply little or no room to accommodate tourists. Accordingly, many kachina dances are off-limits, as is the famous sixteen-day Snake Dance that is held in August.

The kachina masks and dances vary throughout the year, and their timing is determined by close observations of the sun and moon, but their purpose is to intercede with the spirit world to bring health and fertility to pueblo gardens.

The kachinas are several hundred "breath spirits" who live in the nearby San Francisco Peaks. They are not worshiped, but are looked upon as personal friends, the spirits of departed ancestors. The Hopi men perform the kachina dances with the greatest care and respect, preparing for them days in advance. The men chosen to don the spectacular kachina masks regard this as a signal honor and a sacred obligation. To the Hopi, these dances are not merely symbolic. Each dancer, as he puts on his mask, assumes the mask's spirit and *becomes* the kachina. This is as real to the Hopi as the transubstantiation of the bread and wine of the Eucharist is to Roman Catholics.

At the dances where non-Indians are admitted, *bahaana* are asked to respect the kachinas and not applaud, as this is a religious rite. Observers watch the ceremony from the rooftops, or at the edges of the plaza. The splendidly costumed men dance and chant, sending prayers for rain and health back to the kachinas on the San Francisco Peaks. Here are men who work in gardens and shops on the mesa, string telephone wires or lay asphalt while working on road crews, or work construction jobs, who no doubt watch TV, drive around in pickup trucks, and eat counter hamburgers, all lined up and transformed into breath spirits. They sing and dance to keep life in balance with nature.

The Hopi metaphysic, which is called the "Hopi Path" or the "Hopi Way," is at first a little difficult for an outsider to fathom. To the Hopi, all life comes out of a spirit world; each plant and animal, even a passing thunderstorm, has a spirit. This is not exactly animism, where spirits can defy or alter the laws of nature; rather, all laws of nature derive from the spiritual plane of existence. The Hopi Way is based on natural law and the cycles of nature.

At Old Oraibi and at nearby Hotevilla, the Hopi Way is practiced in its purest form. The Hopi are known as the most religious tribe in Arizona. Hotevilla is the most traditional of the independent villages on the mesas. Traditionalists at Old Oraibi broke away from one another in a schism and feud between chiefs in 1906. A line was drawn in the dust, literally, and an actual shoving match ensued, and things got out of hand. The event still looms large in the consciousness of the Hopi—the way 1066 and the Battle of Hastings does in the minds of the British. Driven away, the losers established their own village nearby, calling it Hotevilla. At Hotevilla, you might see one or two TV antennas sticking out of the roofs, a disconcerting sight. But those would be from battery-powered televisions, as Hotevilla's elders, wishing to stick to the old ways, rejected electricity for the entire town.

The name Hopi itself means "good in every way." This has

led to the popular interpretation of Hopi as "the peaceful ones." The name even sounds hopeful. Any definition of a Hopi could have been lifted straight out of the *Boy Scout Handbook*. Hopi are modest, unobtrusive, nonaggressive, morally upright, and keep an even disposition. The name *Hopi* referred not so much to an ethnic or a tribal group as to an attitude and a state of being.

The Hopi Way is revealed in myth and prophecy. The famous Hopi prophecies warn of a world threatened by material temptations and corruptions—a life they call *koyaanisqatsi*. This word has been translated variously as "crazy life," or "life out of balance," or "life disintegrating." The Hopi believe that we are in a fourth and final world, and that only by keeping life in balance with the sublime harmony of nature can the world continue to survive.

In his book *Indian Country*, Peter Matthiessen described how the clan prophecies had been held in secret and handed down to the elders through generations. Matthiessen wrote that after the exodus of the Anasazi from Mesa Verde in Colorado, Maasa'u, or Maasaw, the great spirit or life force, instructed the Hopi to go to these mesas in Arizona and await the arrival of a "True White Brother." He would be a "purifier" who would correct those who had strayed from the Hopi Path or Life Plan. This True White Brother would be recognized by a stone tablet he carried, a match to one given by Maasa'u to the original inhabitants of Old Oraibi, a stone still kept all these centuries by the tribe's spiritual leaders. It wasn't until the atomic bomb was exploded at Alamagordo, New Mexico, in the 1940s that the Hopi decided to reveal to the world their secret clan prophecies. One ancient prophecy seemed to describe the A-bomb itself, warning that "a gourd of ashes might one day fall from the sky, burning the land and boiling waters."

Indian Country is a moving account of the tragedies that have taken, and continue to take, place when white culture intrudes upon the sacred lands of Native Americans. Matthiessen recounted how the Hopi came to grief after first mistaking Spaniards and then Anglos for the True White Brother. The Hopi had to endure missionaries, Indian agents, reservation life, and white-run boarding schools, where white schoolmasters tried to beat the religion, language, and culture out of the Hopi and other Indian children. The traditionalists at such Hopi villages as Old Oraibi and Hotevilla, where the Hopi Way is practiced in its purest forms, have probably done more to resist the white man's materialism than any other Indians in the United States.

Walking around the dusty streets of Old Oraibi, I couldn't help but feel that I was snooping. I wondered how I might react if Indian tourists arrived on my residential block in San Francisco, wanting to examine my apartment and its artifacts. There was a crawling sensation on the back of my neck, as if I were the one who was under observation.

Breath spirits lived up here alongside junker cars and telephone lines. I thought of the Anasazi rock art I had seen down in the canyons; floating anthromorphs with horns, masked figures, quartered circles, reddened handprints, a hunchbacked god playing a flute. What did these symbols signify? Maybe the Hopi are right—our doom is in our materialism. When the TVs go black in Flagstaff and Phoenix, and our civilization breathes its last gasp, perhaps the Hopi will still be up here on their pueblo mesas, praying in the kivas and calling on the kachinas to bless the summer corn.

14

CANYON OF DEATH

I WAS ON the road just outside of Polacca, leaving First Mesa, when I had my first encounter with the concept of Indian time. It occurred at one of those traffic stops where you have to wait to follow a pilot car around some road construction. Usually these stops, common during the summer months, when the highways are under repair, take little more than fifteen minutes to negotiate and are at most minor inconveniences. I waited *one hour and twelve minutes* for the pilot car to show up and lead our stalled caravan a few hundred yards around a single patch of asphalt! The Hopi kid who was holding up the stop sign, smiling and enjoying the scene, explained to me that the road crew was trying to smooth over a bump in the road. Didn't want the *bahaana* bumping their heads when they drove over it. And when would the pilot car show up? Oh, anytime now, anytime.

The road led eastward for fifteen miles to Keams Canyon, named after Thomas Keam, who ran a trading post there in the 1800s. The trading post became a factor in Hopi dependency on a white economy. The easternmost villages on the Hopi mesas, the ones closest to Keams Canyon, were the least traditional of the independently governed villages.

The Hopi used to run on the foot trace between here and Keams and on up to Ganado and to the New Mexican pueblos. The Hopi gardens were connected to one another, and to the clifftop mesas, by a series of dirt footpaths, and the Hopi farmers were always racing back and forth on them. Lewis Tewanima, a Hopi lad, was trained by the legendary coach Glenn "Pop" Warner at the famous Carlisle Indian School in Pennsylvania. A teammate of Jim Thorpe, Tewanima won the silver medal in the ten-thousand-meter race at the 1912 Olympic Games in Stockholm.

Keams Canyon, shared by both the Navajo and the Hopi, houses several federal government offices, a small hospital, a large combined cafeteria and crafts store, and several Christian churches. I stopped at the restaurant and ordered a simple Indian taco for lunch. A name tag identified the cashier as Mark Begay. Mark was apparently my waiter, too. I couldn't quite figure out the cafeteria system. No one seemed to have any one specific job, and I wondered how the food was going to get from the kitchen to my table. But it came in time and it was good, if not delicious. Indian food is very bland but nourishing. And you get a lot at very little cost. My taco was too large even to finish—a mountain of beef, lettuce, cheese, and beans piled onto airy Indian fry bread. I ate, spicing the taco with Tabasco, and I enjoyed watching the cashier and waiters performing different chores at different times with seemingly little in the way of what you would recognize as a system. Was this the ultimate cultural divide between whites and Indians—not race but efficiency? Indians find whites rude, impatient, always in a rush. The name Begay is Navajo. They say you could recognize the physical differences between Navajo and Hopi. The Hopi tend to be a little taller; Navajo men favor wispy mustaches. The

Hopi reservation is entirely surrounded by the much larger Navajo Nation. Trespassing and grazing rights are touchy subjects among them. They are traditional rivals, and yet Navajo and Hopi act more like friends than enemies. I guess they know who their real enemies are.

I CONTINUED EASTWARD through the buff desert until it changed golden and red. I was approaching Canyon de Chelly National Monument, a labyrinth of sculptured sandstone and sheer-walled passages spectacular in their beauty. The canyon once sheltered the mysterious Anasazi. Today, the Navajo make their homes down in the canyon's cottonwood bottoms.

I set up my tent in Cottonwood Campground, not far from the visitor's center. The sparse cottonwoods provided little shelter from the wind. Signs posted prominently warned campers not to leave gear unattended. There were also warnings forbidding soliciting in the campground, a posting I had not seen before in any national park or monument. I wondered what was really meant by "soliciting"—panhandling, more likely. The presence of rangers in the camp was highly visible. At other parks, their presence had been less obtrusive. I watched a ranger accompany the campground host on his rounds. The pair were taking a careful written inventory of who and what was in camp. I was picking up some very bad vibes.

The western entrance to the canyon begins not far from the town of Chinle. At first, the canyon walls are only a few feet high, but the gorge soon deepens dramatically. Two main arms of the canyon divided early on. I followed the paved road south along a rim a thousand feet above the canyon floor.

Visitors are confined principally to the overlooks. If you want to go down into the canyon, you have to hire a Navajo guide. And you need a four-wheel-drive vehicle. There are no paved roads down there. I pulled into the parking lot at Tsegi

Overlook. Far down below me, I could see automobiles plow-
ing through the shallow waters of the wash. The scene looked
oddly hilarious. I counted a few tiny houses and patch farms
among the green cottonwoods. Peach trees were in bloom. Up
on the overlook, Navajo hawked cheap trinkets and schlock
jewelry. Many had small children with them. Their display
blankets were spread out on the asphalt next to their pickup
trucks. Their wares looked incredibly chintzy.

Although most of the canyon bottom is off-limits to visitors
without guides, the one exception is the trail to the White
House Ruin. I had planned to make that two-hour hike. But
when I got to the White House Ruin Overlook, signs warned
visitors against leaving their cars unattended, as break-ins were
occurring with alarming frequency, even in broad daylight. All
my gear was in my car. A rip-off would abort my trip. I took
a good look around and saw graffiti scrawled on signs and on
the pavement. Now here was a first for a national monument:
The scrawlings appeared to be gang signs.

I enjoyed touring the canyon overlooks on the south rim,
gazing down at faraway Anasazi ruins set into the alcoves of
towering canyon walls and watching the big Detroit steel of
Navajo vehicles pushing their way through the shallow waters
of Chinle Wash. Red canyon cliffs rose straight up to an incredible height, overshadowing the streams, cottonwoods, and
small farms.

Spider Rock rises up over the confluence of Canyon de
Chelly and Monument Canyon. The Navajo once used this
high, narrow split rock as a lookout. Its needle silhouette makes
it the most striking sandstone formation in the canyon. Navajo
parents are said to warn children that Spider Woman will take
them to her rock and eat them if they don't behave. Or so the
Navajo guides have been telling tourists for years. This story
doesn't wash. Spider Woman is a benevolent figure in Navajo

mythology. She gave birth to a number of deities and taught Navajo women how to weave. The Navajo enjoy putting on the *belagana*, so perhaps the story had been invented for the tourist trade.

No other place on the Colorado Plateau has been occupied for as long by Indians as Canyon de Chelly. They have been living here, relatively uninterrupted, for the past five thousand years. Paleo-Indians left no permanent dwellings, but remains of their campsites are still found, as are their pictographs and petroglyphs. Later, the Basket Maker people constructed pit compounds, as well as building granaries high on the canyon walls where the food would be well protected. The Basket Makers were succeeded by the Anasazi, who built pueblos—compound multistory households with kivas.

About seven hundred years ago, most of the Anasazi drifted away, but a few stayed behind. Later, their ancestors, migrating Hopis, and other Southwestern tribes visited the canyon in the summer to hunt and farm. Finally, at the end of a long migration, the Navajo arrived, and they have been here ever since. Like the Indians who came before them, the Navajo probably moved up to the canyon rims during winter, when shorter days left the canyon dark and gloomy. They built forked-stick hogans, the openings facing the east for sunrise, and added their own art to the canyon walls. Modern Navajo continue to live in the canyon only during the spring and summer months. They make their homes above the canyon the rest of the year.

The labyrinth known as Canyon de Chelly is really several canyons. The name Canyon de Chelly is derived from Spanish. The Navajo called their canyon Tsegi, a generic Navajo term for "canyon" or "canyon of rocks." There are two main branches cut by many side canyons. Sometime toward evening, I made the long drive north toward the other main branch, Canyon del Muerto, the Canyon of Death. It was late—the overlook parking lot was deserted. Signs warned against leaving unattended vehicles. Vandals had defaced the signs and pavement with graffiti.

The Canyon of Death got its name from a rather sordid massacre that occurred here in 1805. After a relatively tranquil period of Navajo occupation in Canyon de Chelly, sporadic warfare broke out between the Navajo and Spanish colonists in the nearby Rio Grande Valley. Reprisals followed raids as the Navajo clashed with the Spanish and other Southwestern tribes over land and grazing room. The Navajo used Canyon de Chelly as a fortress refuge, where they thought they'd be invincible.

They were wrong. It was one thing to ward off Ute raiders armed with bows and arrows, but quite another thing to repel Spanish horsemen armed with rifles. A lieutenant named Antonio Narbona led a raiding party of Spanish horsemen into Canyon del Muerto in the winter of 1804–1805. Narbona trapped the Navajo in high caves. Thousands of bullets were fired; the ricochet marks can still be seen on the walls of what has come to be known as Massacre Cave. The Navajo didn't have a chance. Narbona sent proof of his victory back to the capital at Santa Fe—a package containing severed ears, with an apology for six missing pairs. Narbona reported killing "ninety warriors, twenty-five women and children." The Navajo said Narbona's men actually killed mostly women, children, the elderly, and the sick.

Spanish control of what is now Arizona and New Mexico came to an end in 1846 as the result of United States military campaigns in that region. Two years later, after the conclusion of the Mexican War and the signing of the Treaty of Guadalupe Hidalgo, the land that is now the American Southwest formally passed hands from Mexico to the United States. Over the next seventeen years, continued conflicts, broken promises, and numerous white incursions into Navajo territory tested relations between the United States and the Navajo. Military posts were set up throughout the Southwest to protect white settlers. In 1863, Gen. James H. Carleton, the U.S. territorial commander in New Mexico, decided that the troublesome Navajo had to be subdued, rounded up, and packed off to a reservation in the badlands near Bosque Redondo to learn Christianity and agriculture. He knew just the man to get the job done—Kit Carson. Col. Christopher "Kit" Carson was a famous frontiersman, who had been a close friend to the Dineh, and he knew intimately their ways and culture. Under orders from Carleton and the territorial government, Kit Carson launched a brutal campaign against his old friends. Angry Hopi, Ute, and Zuni joined up with Carson as scouts to get in their licks against their old enemies.

It was a "scorched earth" campaign. Bands of Navajo fled before the oncoming bluecoats, many hiding in the the northern canyon country. Like Sherman marching on Atlanta, Carson's troops burned the Navajo's hogans, slaughtered their sheep, and destroyed their crops and fields.

In January 1864, Carson arrived at the mouth of Canyon de Chelly, where many of the Navajo were holed up, demoralized and starving. Carson knew the area well from earlier reconnaissance missions to the canyon. His bluecoats entered the canyon from its deep eastern end, pushing the Navajo toward the canyon's mouth. A few were killed; others were captured. The remainder, cold and hungry, and lured by promises of food and shelter, gave themselves up. Later that spring, Carson returned to the canyon to complete the devastation, destroying the remaining hogans and sheep and burning five thousand peach trees under cultivation by the Navajo. To this day, the Navajo still talk about those burned peach trees.

The army had their Navajo captives penned up at Fort Defi-

144 · MICHAEL CHECCHIO

ance. They ordered all 8,500 of them to make a forced march of more than three hundred miles to the badlands of southeastern New Mexico for permanent relocation near Bosque Redondo. This was the infamous Long Walk, the bitterest chapter in Navajo history. Those who survived the march couldn't adapt to the bareness and inhumane conditions, and they begged to return home. After four years, the United States relented. But the Navajo never forgot their betrayal by Kit Carson.

It was an uneasy truce. In time, army distribution centers gave way to trading posts on the reservation. The posts served as both dry-goods stores and cultural-exchange centers. Indian traders became counselors to the Navajo. They opened up markets for native folk craft. Sheepherding became even more important as the Navajo discovered buyers for their wool. In time, reservation schools were built. The Navajo had a facility for adapting cultural changes they liked into their own traditions.

World War II brought the first large exodus from the reservation in modern times. Young Navajo men served with distinction in the armed services. The most famous unit was the Navajo Code Talkers—420 Navajo marines who used a code based on the Navajo language to broadcast vital military transmissions in the Pacific theater. The invasion of Iwo Jima, among other campaigns, was directed by orders sent over shortwave radios in static bursts of Navajo. The Japanese found it impossible to break the code; they couldn't even guess the language. Today, those surviving Code Talkers are among the most revered of Navajo elders.

When the Navajo returned home from their military service and wartime jobs, they brought back information and ideas from the outside. In all, the Navajo had to absorb many cultural shocks. They had been forced to make the leap from a so-called primitive society to a modern one in something less than a lifetime.

From an empty overlook, I stared down into the loneliness of Canyon del Muerto. These days, only about thirty Navajo families live down in Canyon de Chelly. They have a hard time finding relatives available to work the family farms in the summer. Most Navajo live above the rim or in nearby Chinle, their traditional hogans standing next to modern ranch houses. They can't get away from their full-time jobs, so they live year-round above the rim. Of course, they like to use the summer hogans in the canyon for vacations and holidays.

Tourism is a thriving business here. The cafeteria inside Thunderbird Lodge was once a part of the historic trading post built by the Indian trader Sam Day. Thunderbird Lodge operates Thunderbird Tours, which offers guided excursions into the canyon in specially adapted all-terrain vehicles.

Returning to the campground, I noticed something about my neighbors that had not been evident at other parks. This campground was full of Navajo. There they were with their large families, crammed into Winnebagos and Airstreams, sitting at picnic tables enjoying their evening meal. Canyon de Chelly had become a destination for Navajo tourists.

WE WHITES HAVE constantly reinvented Indians in our own minds. Once we needed to believe that Indians were bloodthirsty savages in order to justify manifest destiny. Then they became the noble red man of John Ford films. Today, they are either environmentalists or spiritual icons. We bend history to fit an evolving notion we have, not about other people, but about ourselves.

There is another role they have sometimes played, and played too well—the drunken Indian. I was standing outside a Laundromat in Chinle one morning, waiting for my wash to complete the spin cycle, when a middle-aged Navajo man ambled up to me in the parking lot. With bloodshot eyes, long, greasy black hair, he wore the kind of soiled jumpsuit a mechanic might wear.

"*Ya at eeh,*" he hailed me brightly, a front tooth missing from his broad grin. He was hungover, but putting a good face on the morning. I had a feeling he was about to become my new best friend.

"*Yaat a hey,*" I said.

"No. *Ya AAAT eeh,*" he said, placing the accent on the second syllable and drawing it out to make it sound positively exuberant. Great. I had mispronounced the one Navajo phrase I thought I knew. So much for trying to use Tony Hillerman novels as a Berlitz primer.

"I wrecked my car the other night," my new acquaintance told me straight off. "I rolled it into a ditch. I don't know what I'm going to do without that car."

I was about to be hit up for some spare change. He knew I knew it, and he seemed a little embarrassed by it. But that didn't stop my new friend from offering to teach me a few phrases of Navajo. And although he taught me how to say good-bye in his native tongue, I knew there would be no saying good-bye to Hoskee "Tony" Burbank until he was ready to leave.

I had read in Tony Hillerman's novels that the American habit of interrupting a person in midconversation is impolite to the Navajo. And so I paused in respectful silence each time Tony told me something. This way, he would know I was listening carefully and politely considering everything he said. But Tony expected me to comment instantly on every damn thing he told me—his drinking habits and his car accident, for example—and he kept insisting I tell him what was on my mind—which, I answered truthfully, was nothing, as Tony was a bit hard to fathom.

"What do you do?" Tony asked me. I made the mistake of

telling him I was a writer. "I'll tell you my story," he offered. "Native Americans don't lie." He suggested a gratuity of a few bucks might be in order.

Tony, who told me he was forty-nine years old, was raised not on the reservation but in Glendale, near Los Angeles. There were more Navajo in LA than anywhere outside the Navajo reservation. More Navajo in LA than in Gallup, New Mexico. Tony said he started drinking when he was in Salt Lake City and that was his downfall. He had been to Salt Lake, Denver, "all over" the West, and now he was living on the rez near Chinle. He said everything was "free" out here; he didn't have to pay any taxes. "Land of the free," he said.

A Navajo woman managing the Laundromat, the one who had given me quarters for the machines, walked over and glowered at Tony. Tony, who was obviously well-known in this establishment, was about to get the bum's rush.

"He's writing a book," Tony told her. "I'm telling him my life story and he's going to put it in a book." The woman looked at me as if to say this couldn't possibly be true, and what kind of a fool was I, anyway? Tony looked highly satisfied with himself for not getting eighty-sixed.

"Where are you going next?" Tony asked me. I felt a twinge of alarm at this question. This guy planned to attach himself to me.

"New Mexico," I lied.

"I know this country around here real good," Tony said. "I can take you into canyons nobody goes into."

"Sorry, Tony, I'm going to New Mexico. I'm going to visit my sisters." Tony persisted, still trying to talk me into hiring him as a guide. But he gave up when he saw I wasn't going to budge. He asked me if I could spare just a little more change.

"Sorry, Tony, I'm tapped out."

Finally, after one final elocution lesson, Tony and I bid a

friendly farewell to each other, saying good-bye in Navajo, in a phrase I promptly forgot. And judging by Tony's laughter, that was probably a good thing, because my pronunciation was all screwed up. Tony made a point of shaking my hand. I had read somewhere that Indians usually don't shake hands with one another, finding the custom faintly ridiculous. Perhaps Tony was having me on—or maybe just being genuinely friendly.

Tony shuffled across the parking lot. Being a Navajo wasn't all corn pollen and eagle feathers. It hadn't been easy in this century for the Navajo to maintain *hozho* and walk in beauty. There are many reasons given—historical, sociological, and otherwise—for the destructive drinking habits of so many Native Americans. Grief, anger, despair, and the frustration of losing their land and culture no doubt are at the root of it.

I gathered my laundry and drove over to the Navajo Chapter House, where there were public showers, but it was Sunday and the place was closed.

Where was I going anyway? Hoskee "Tony" Burbank had wanted to know, and I had lied to him. Immediately, I knew where I was heading.

New Mexico.

15

G H O S T S

OVER THE MOUNTAIN pass into New Mexico. I had passed through Tsaile, Arizona, where the community college is shaped like a traditional eight-sided hogan, its entrance facing east toward the sunrise. And then up into the Chuska Mountains, their slopes covered in a dark mantle of fir and lodgepole. Navajo men fished on a wind-chopped lake. The cooling pines brought relief from the red desert. Cresting the fragrant green mountains, I gazed down into an incredible panorama—the tan platform of the New Mexican badlands.

Tumbleweeds whipped across the highway and my Chevy Blazer rocked in the crosswinds. Everyone seemed to be going too fast or too slow, especially the Navajo in their fishtailing cars and rattletrap pickups. It felt very dangerous and threatening out here. Striking rock outcroppings rose up in the distance over stark, flat badlands. The *bitsi*, or badlands, of the Four Corners region—Tony Hillerman country.

I listened to the latest news reports coming over the radio. A Navajo medicine man was coming to Hovenweep to perform a purification ceremony. The shaman was going to bless the ground around the house where the park ranger had been shot at by the renegade survivalists, who were still on the lam. The manhunt for the fugitives was still going strong in the Four Corners region. The shaman was coming to Hovenweep to undo some of the sacrilege. The radio report was unclear on whether the Navajo medicine man was going to perform his rituals among the actual Anasazi sites at Hovenweep. I thought it unlikely. Traditional Navajo steer clear of Anasazi ruins, believing the ancestral sites of their enemies to be powerful places, under the spell of witchcraft. These sites are *chindi*—"haunted."

The great volcanic plug of Shiprock rose up on my left. White settlers called the high, sharp pinnacle Ship Rock because its shape reminded them of a ship in full sail. The Navajo called the mountain Tsebitai, or Winged Rock, likening it to a great bird. It worked either way. Navajo belief held that the bird carried the Dineh to New Mexico. This mass of dark lava rock, rising fourteen hundred feet above the flat desert, once had filled the cone of a volcano. Over time, the volcano eroded away, leaving only the plug. Like everything out here in the Four Corners region, it looked highly mysterious and just a little spooky.

I passed the town of Shiprock, noticing signs for hospitals and medical clinics. Just like at Chinle, medical clinics seemed to predominate. That's because in Indian country too many people were either sick or had something seriously wrong with them. Hanta virus had broken out on the rez. Bubonic plague was not just something you read about in history books on medieval Europe. Fetal alcohol syndrome cursed generations of Navajo children. Drunkenness, poverty, and violence were endemic. Navajo tribal police were being murdered while trying to patrol the far-flung distances of their reservation. These lone officers had no backup, no one to come to their assistance when they were shot at. Tribal teens were drinking suicidally and killing one another in acts of sheer nihilism. It was a tragedy of inestimable dimension.

On past the New Mexican towns of Shiprock and Farmington, across the border into southwestern Colorado. At Cortez, I turned east on the road to Durango, on up the highway that rises out of the desert into forested highlands.

The spirits of the ancient ones haunt the Southwest. And nowhere is their presence more strongly felt than on Mesa Verde. Here are perhaps the most splendid Indian cliff dwellings in North America. When the Spaniards got here, they called this high plateau Mesa Verde, or the Green Table. As many as two thousand years ago, Indians were attracted to the forested slopes of this verdant tableland. All the elements seemed to be in balance up here.

The Anasazi succeeded the Basket Makers, occupying Mesa Verde over a period of seven hundred years. In the last century of their occupation, they built magnificent stone cities, setting them into cliffside overhangs and alcoves in the steep canyons that cut the tableland into finger mesas. And then quite abruptly, and mysteriously, they abandoned their cities and migrated south to New Mexico and Arizona. Why the Anasazi left Mesa Verde so suddenly remains one of the great enigmas of the Southwest.

White men first chanced upon the Anasazi ruins of Mesa Verde in the winter of 1888, when a pair of cowboys from the nearby Mancos Valley, Richard Wetherill and his brother-in-law Charles Mason, rode to the top of the mesa in an effort to round up stray cattle. At the edge of a juniper and piñon forest lay a vast canyon, the same canyon I was staring at from the overlook. The only difference was that Wetherill and his brother-in-law were across the canyon on the other side, near Sun Temple. Through blowing snow, they could distinguish something in the cliffs that looked like "a magnificent city."

They became the first white men to see what they would later name Cliff Palace, the largest cliff dwelling in North America. Over two decades, Wetherill and Mason would return with three of Richard's brothers to explore Cliff Palace and discover other nearby ruins on Mesa Verde. Tourist parties and other exploratory groups followed. There was much looting of artifacts and visitors were not shy about defacing the ruins. In 1906, in an effort to protect the Anasazi sites, Congress made Mesa Verde a national park and formal excavations and restorations began to be carried out under the direction of the Smithsonian Institution.

In order to visit Cliff Palace, I would have to violate my rule about not taking conducted tours. But I had no choice. And so by midafternoon, I found myself with fifty or sixty other tourists gathered near the canyon rim overlooking Cliff Palace, listening to a park ranger give his canned lecture and repeat the same cornball jokes that no doubt he would be telling a thousand times before the season ended. Our ranger dutifully tried to warn those among us with bad hearts and respiratory ailments from descending into the canyon with him. The rangers didn't want tourists stroking out on them.

We followed our ranger buddy down the steep trail to Cliff Palace, marveling at the sandstone village. "Cliff Palace," the ranger informed us, "contained two hundred and seventeen rooms and twenty-three kivas. As you can see, the main construction material here is sandstone. The Anasazi chipped this softer sandstone with riverbed stones that they used as hammers." Our ranger asked us to note the stone chinking that the Anasazi used to fill in the gaps and reinforce walls that had been cemented together with a mortar mixture of mud and water. "The doorways were kept deliberately small," he explained, "in order to keep out the cold air and drafts in winter."

A few wooden beams protruded from the walls. These were

the last of the original reinforcing timbers. By taking core samples from the logs, then counting the number of annual tree rings, anthropologists were able to date Cliff Palace to the thirteenth century. The tree rings showed that Cliff Palace had been a work in progress, from 1209 through the 1270s. As the population increased in size, the Anasazi built on. They were constantly adding or removing walls and remodeling doorways, making them smaller or blocking them up. The Anasazi had to carry all their water up to the city. The nearest spring lay on the other side of the canyon, below Sun Temple. That was a long haul—but perhaps worth it for the million-dollar views. There's no reason to doubt that the Anasazi, living in this cave-like niche high above the canyon floor, were any less in love with scenery than we are today.

We came upon an open kiva, a large circular chamber, the ceremonial room of the Anasazi. Based upon what we know of the Hopi living on their mesa-top villages in Arizona, we can deduce that these kivas also functioned as lodge houses. Like the modern-day Hopi, the Anasazi used their kivas for religious ceremonies and social gatherings and even as weaving rooms. I counted six stone pilasters on the inside walls that had once helped support the original roof, which was now missing. The roof would have served as part of a courtyard above. The Indians would have entered the kiva by way of a ladder in the center of the roof. The base of the ladder would have rested directly above the fire pit. I assumed this meant an occasional scorched behind. A low wall of stones had been built a few feet away from the fire pit to serve as a deflector for the heat. Smoke rose through the roof hatchway, and the partial vacuum this created drew fresh air down a ventilator shaft located within the stones of a south-facing recess. The pilasters rested upon a stone banquette, a benchlike shelf that could have been used for storage. In the inner walls of the kiva were rectangular niches that might have held ornaments, eagle and turkey feathers, and other ceremonial objects. In my mind, I tried to picture what it was like here seven hundred years ago, with the ancestral Pueblos conducting their healing rites, praying for rain and success in hunting.

I noticed a small crease in the floor between the fire pit and the north-facing wall. This was the symbolic entrance to the underworld, the *sipapu*, a spirit hole.

They lived in Cliff Palace only a short time, maybe seventy-five years. And then by 1300, Mesa Verde was entirely deserted. Cliff Palace, the Long House, Far View, the Spruce Tree House—all were abandoned. Tree rings indicated a great drought occurred between 1276 and the end of the thirteenth century. But the Anasazi of Mesa Verde had survived droughts before. Perhaps the soil and forests gave out. Maybe the Anasazi had social and political problems. Maybe they were threatened by invaders. The reason for their migration is not known. In any case, the Anasazi and other ancients were always making unexplained departures. For whatever reason, the Anasazi of Mesa Verde abruptly migrated south to New Mexico and Arizona, settling among their kin there. Many modern-day Pueblo Indians, such as the Hopi, are direct descendants of the cliff dwellers of Mesa Verde.

Let us say the Anasazi left Mesa Verde because of drought, the most common explanation. Does it make sense that they would have resettled in an even more arid land? Why abandon the splendid aeries of Colorado for the rather bleak mesas of Arizona or the dry heat of New Mexico? Why give up those cool summers and million-dollar views?

I prefer the answer suggested by the Australian novelist Thomas Keneally. In the travel book he wrote on the American Southwest, *The Place Where Souls Are Born*, the author of *Schindler's List* meditated upon the disappearance of the Anasazi from Mesa Verde. Keneally wrote that the Anasazi believed that drought was evidence of a world that was failing them. Not just the physical world, but the spiritual one, too. For the Anasazi, droughts were more than just acts of nature—they were signs that the metaphysical universe was disintegrating. Disasters didn't happen by chance; they were evidence of a disordered world. And when that world failed them, they moved. Keneally wondered if perhaps the Anasazi were rejecting the materialism and social complexity of their growing cities. And the novelist imagined a people inspired by a visionary leader—an Indian Moses or a Brigham Young—who led them on an exodus out of the cities and into the desert so they might undergo a spiritual purification. The departure from Mesa Verde might have been a healing act. Of all the reasons given for the Anasazi migration, this is the one that most appeals to me.

I DROVE UP to Park Point, highest elevation on the mesa. There I was met with an unobstructed panorama of four states, one of the grandest and most extensive views I have ever seen.

The air was exceptionally clear, with no hint of man-made or natural haze. I could see more than a hundred miles away, as far away as the La Sal Mountains in Utah and the Lukachukais in Arizona. The view to the north revealed Lone Cone, Mount Wilson, and the Dolores Peaks some fifty miles away, all part of the San Juans, the southernmost group of the great Rocky Mountains.

On the east lay the forested Mancos Valley, bordered by the La Plata Mountains and Menefee Mountain. On the southern horizon, the volcanic plug of Shiprock rose up out of the New Mexican desert, and, farther south, I could make out another fantastic outcropping, the Hogback Mountains. Fifty miles away in Arizona, the Carrizos were visible, and, fifty miles beyond them, the dim outline of the Lukachukais. On the immediate western horizon over in Utah lay Sleeping Ute Mountain. As I looked closely and concentrated, I could see that the mountain did indeed resemble a sleeping figure. There was its head resting toward the north, face gazing up at the sky. Toward the south, the formation indicated folded arms across a chest, then thighs, knees, and feet. The western view seemed to run out endlessly toward the Abajos and the Manti–La Sal National Forest.

The Anasazi had stood at this very place, on the rooftop of their world, and gazing west and south, looking out at the same views I was beholding, they decided to leave their green forests and disperse into the great buff- and rust-colored wastelands waiting for them in the distances. I wondered what it would feel like to embark on such a soul journey.

I set up my tent at a campground seventeen miles from the cliff dwellings on Chapin Mesa. I was surrounded by thickets of Gambel oak and I soon found out I wasn't alone. A family of mule deer, a doe and three fawns, browsed in the forest nearby. They were alert but unafraid. I watched them for a long time. They drew ever closer to my campsite. Finally, the doe walked over. She stood right next to the picnic table, directly across from me, and looked at me with huge liquid brown eyes. I could have reached out across that table and touched her had I chosen to. She probably would have let me.

16

TROUT FISHING IN NEW MEXICO

A TROUT RIVER runs through the barren New Mexican desert. It has no business being there. The San Juan River heads in the breathtaking Rocky Mountains of southwestern Colorado; flowing into the badlands of New Mexico, it becomes Navajo Lake, a reservoir of equally breathtaking ugliness.

For a few miles downstream of Navajo Dam, which holds back the lake, the San Juan becomes trouty. The lake behind the dam chills what would otherwise be a warm, silt-laden desert stream. Gone here are the floods of spring and the low-water droughts of late summer and autumn. The dam releases a steady flow of water from the bottom of the lake, at a bone-chilling 43°F all year, creating ideal habitat conditions for trout.

The fish immediately below the dam are rainbow trout of trophy size, up to twenty-four inches in length, with black-and-emerald backs that camouflage them against a mossy bottom. Brown trout appear a little farther downstream as the water is gradually warmed by the desert. The river continues to warm farther downstream and hosts a mixed population of brown, rainbow, and cutthroat trout.

The trout fishery is a short one. The desert soon reclaims its own. Ten brief miles below the dam, the river becomes a desert stream once again, silty and warm, home to sculpins. The San Juan flows on, picking up the tributaries of Mancos River, the Rio Animas (River of Souls), and the Chaco; crosses the badlands of the Four Corners; flows northwest into Navajoland and the Mormon country of Utah; descends into its most tortuous stretch, a winding gorge known as the Goosenecks; and comes out at the dead-water impoundment of Lake Powell.

In the canyon below Navajo Dam, scores of trout fishermen could be seen wading the river when I was there. The water was cold and a little high, although mostly wadable for fishermen. The combination of hot desert sun and cold water creates vast beds of moss where insects hatch year-round. These mossy beds and weed lines attract trout that feed greedily on midge pupae. Big fish were visible on the bottom, most of them rainbows between seventeen and twenty inches in length. Even in the shallow stretches, refracting light and riffled currents made it difficult to spot fish camouflaged against the luxuriant moss.

I have been a fly fisherman for the better part of my adult life, and I know that what some people call an art is really little more than a method. There is nothing artistic about fly-fishing, nothing particularly creative about it, nothing to elevate it over any other kind of fishing. But for the last quarter of a century, it has been not only my obsession to fly-fish but my delight.

We consider fishing a sport, but in a sport, both sides know you're playing a game. We fish for pleasure, although there's surely little pleasure in it for the fish. Trout probably don't process pain and discomfort like humans—they have no cerebral cortex to speak of—but they react in what we might call panic, and if a trout could talk, I doubt the word *sporting* would enter its vocabulary at the moment the hook was set. In Yellowstone

National Park in Wyoming, where I sometimes go trout fishing, you are not allowed to lasso an elk or a buffalo for sport and pull it around the meadow. Nor can you tie a string onto an eagle and fly it like a kite. But in Yellowstone, where you cannot so much as feed a squirrel a peanut, where the wildlife is supposedly protected from all interference by humans, you are free to hook a trout in the mouth, jerk it out of its watery habitat, and hold it in your hands, if only to revive it and let it go, in most cases. That is the rule and it is called "no kill" or "catch and release." And so I catch and release; and I no longer kill and eat the trout I catch. I go through the ritual of a hunt one step removed from its reality. I try to turn life into a metaphorical experience, but often I wonder why I torment these dumb animals that I truly love. Yet I have no intention of ever giving up fishing. Trout fishing may be one of the few things that keeps me level. For me, it opens all kinds of doors into mystery. It is a way I reach the invisible plane on the other side of the visible world.

I had driven down from Mesa Verde back into the Four Corners region with the express intention of fishing the San Juan River at Navajo Dam. Trout fishermen from all over North America and even Asia and Europe come here to test their fly-fishing skills. Those who drive the dusty desert roads and follow the signs come to Navajo Dam (the town). Those, like me, who aren't paying close attention arrive at Navajo Dam (the dam). The dam is perhaps half a mile across—a massive wall of cement closing off the head of a canyon. Highway 539 runs across the top of the span. A concrete spillway at one end of the dam releases water into the San Juan. From high above this span, I gazed on the panorama of the river below. As the San Juan entered the canyon from the spillway, it swept wide to the right and channeled out among many low islands. All the room in the world for a back cast down there. I would certainly not feel hemmed-in fishing down below. I backtracked to Navajo Dam (the town), where there seemed to be more fly shops than bars, a bad sign in any community.

I BOUGHT A seven-day nonresident New Mexico fishing license at a shop called Duranglers and paid a day-use fee to utilize the stretch of the river that ran through a state park directly downstream of the dam. I followed the turnoff on a canyon side road marked by a church and came to a sprawling parking lot already half-full. Out in the river, dozens of fly fishermen were playing with their flies.

Several well-worn paths led through willows and brush to the riverbank. Signs caution fishermen to leave the water when they hear an air-raid siren, a warning that a hydro release is imminent. The canyon's high northern wall is set well back from the river, a sandstone palisade dotted with sage and juniper.

I waded out into the wide, willow-bordered river. All around me, fly fishermen were drifting tiny artificial flies under brightly colored strike indicators. They had attached split shot onto their leaders in order to sink their weightless flies. The idea was to fish tiny midge imitations near the bottom, where the rainbow trout were feeding. I spotted pods of fish wiggling side by side under the rippling current. The river was a combination of riffles and deeper runs, with several shallow side currents braiding around clumps of islands. These islands range in size from a few square yards to half an acre or more. Pods of trout had gathered in feeding lanes created by the flows around the islands and in the shallower side channels. These trout seemed aware, although little concerned, of the presence of many anglers wading among them. Occasionally, a trout would flip its tail and push away from the gravel to avoid a wading fisherman. All the anglers, men and women, were dressed in hundreds of dollars' worth of fly-fishing livery. And nobody was catching anything but weeds.

Except for two guys. These two young fellows seemed to be cleaning up and fishing rings around everyone else. This pair seemingly had solved the unified field theory of the San Juan. One of these young men appeared to my eyes to be a Navajo; he had long black hair, copper skin, a wispy mustache, and faintly Oriental features. Like many Navajo, he looked like a Mongolian cowboy. He was catching trout on what seemed to be every sixth or seventh cast. And like a movie Indian, he was downright stoic about it. He showed no emotion whatsoever— just released his fish and calmly lit another cigarette. Which was a remarkable act of detachment for a guy hooking trophy-size trout. His companion was doing even better than he was. He wasn't quite so cool about it, though; he kept looking up to see if anyone was watching, which everyone was. Like his companion, he, too, had Oriental features, but that was because he was Korean and not Navajo, as I would learn later. He was catching huge, flopping trout on every third or fourth cast. And he had reduced it to a routine.

The trout these men caught were exceptionally large, four or five pounds apiece, true dream trout. But there was something unnatural about these trout, too, and it took me awhile to figure out just what was out of place. Rainbow trout that big and strong should have been tearing off the line and turning cartwheels in the air. The water should have been boiling and flying all around them. They should have been spooling the anglers. Rainbow trout are aerial acrobats by nature, a mixture of strength and explosive grace. But these San Juan trout wouldn't jump. Nor would they make line-burning runs. Instead, when hooked, they thrashed a bit and then swam in a tight circle until the initial unpleasantness of being hooked wore off; then they simply surrendered. These fish knew they were about to be released! It wasn't the artificially chill temperature of the river that was slowing down their metabolisms, making them sluggish, which is what I thought at first. These fish had been caught and released so many times, they knew the drill. These San Juan beauties had stopped behaving like true rainbow trout. They had adjusted to the presence of thousands of fishermen over time and were simply not behaving like wild animals anymore. I had seen this adaptive behavior before, with cutthroat trout at Buffalo Ford on the Yellowstone River in Yellowstone National Park, where your average cutthroat is caught and released dozens of times a season.

"Well, you're certainly the best fly fisherman I've seen on this river," I told the young Korean fellow when he waded up close beside me. He had just caught and released what must have been his thirtieth trout. He had been, as they say, emptying the pool.

"People either love me or hate me," he said with a laugh. He introduced himself as Andy Kim, a professional guide. He was on the river trying to drum up some clients. He showed me his rig: a tiny dark midge imitation attached to a gossamer tippet with a bit of split shot. The trick was to fish the fly at just the right depth where the fish fed, and Andy knew exactly where that depth was to be found at any given time in the river's cycle of pupae and mayfly emergence. And he made it clear that anyone could be similarly successful if only they had the clarity of mind to hire him as a guide.

"I've fished the Green River," he said, "the San Juan, all over Colorado. I just got back from the Yukon. Look on the Internet and you'll find me. I'm all over the Internet."

Andy told me he had been born in Korea. He was making a career as a fly fisherman and a river guide in the Southwest. Later, in the parking lot, Andy showed me his scrapbook. There was a published article on the San Juan that referred to this trout hustler as "the infamous Andy Kim." Infamous because he caught trout the way a carpet sweeper picks up lint. Andy told me that other fishermen on the San Juan, including some of the guides who worked out of the local fly shops, resented him, but he dismissed this as simple jealousy. He was affable, had a true love of his sport, and obviously was a brilliant angler. And he was everything that had gone wrong with fly-fishing over the past twenty years.

What was once the pastime of iconoclasts and true amateurs has turned competitive, self-promotional, and in a few cases lucrative. Fly-fishing has become a big business. Fly shops routinely hold streamside "seminars" that cost more than what I paid for a semester of comparative lit back when I was in college. A new graphite rod at today's prices would set me back more than what I paid for my first car, a very dependable used Ford. Blue-ribbon trout streams such as the San Juan have filled up with status seekers, professional hustlers, and egos as big as the great outdoors.

For me, fly-fishing is about mystery. I didn't need this scene in the parking lot; I didn't need this circus on the San Juan. What I wanted was a wilderness experience, and I wasn't going to get one on the San Juan River below Navajo Dam.

On the San Juan, I seemed to be fishing in a state of cognitive dissonance. I was standing with my fellow anglers downstream from a desperately ugly hydroelectric dam, hip-deep in a river that rose and fell not with nature's cycles but like a flushing toilet, fly-fishing for trout in a place where trout shouldn't exist at all, trying to hook non-native rainbows that wouldn't jump or perform in the way nature meant rainbow trout to act.

Modern society has advanced to the stage where it has effectively distanced itself from the elemental world. And the feelings and states of being that I was after were getting harder to find. I fished until the sun slipped behind the canyon wall and the air grew chilly. I caught nothing, which was okay—I don't need to catch fish, only know that they are there. But there was an unreality to these badlands. The cold blue water looked out of place among drab desert cliffs. Everything was taking on interesting tones in the evening's half-light, but the river hadn't won my soul.

EARLY THE NEXT morning, I drove eastward over the dusty badlands into the rolling green highlands of New Mexico. I listened to Navajo Nation radio from Farmington until the signal faded. The Native American music came as a welcome relief from country-and-western schlock, and the news broadcasts were leavened by ironic political commentary and interesting community chat about the rez. I listened to the latest news bulletins on the search for the outlaw fugitives: Law-enforcement authorities had set fire to more brushy bank cover along the San Juan River well below where I had been fishing, where it flowed into Utah, in a second attempt to smoke the gunmen out of hiding. I thought that was a bit of overkill, but I knew it would do little harm to the environment. That brush can always use a good fire.

After the hot buff desert, the highlands of northern New Mexico came as a relief. The pine forests felt refreshing. The pastures and horse ranches were deep in blue grama grasses. Narrow streams ran out of the pine green hills, racing over stony riffles and gravelly bottoms, twisting through brilliant meadows and forests of blue pine and mixed conifer. Fly-fishing was said to be good in many spots along the little Chama, so I decided to make camp near its brushy banks.

An old railroad depot lured tourists to the picture-postcard town of Chama. A high trestle bridge spanned the river. The coal-fired Cumbres & Toltec Scenic Railroad, the longest and highest narrow-gauge coal-burning steam train in the United States, made runs daily between Chama and Osier, Colorado, departing every morning from mid-May through mid-October. I had lunch at the Whistle Stop Cafe near the railroad museum and then began asking around the souvenir shops and sporting-goods stores for good tips on the local fly-fishing.

I wound up fifteen miles south of Chama, near Tierra Amarilla, looking for a way onto the Brazos River. The Brazos flows mostly through private ranch land. The river had a pair of fishing lodges, as well as a bunch of new vacation homes going up under the pines at the head of the canyon. Land was mostly posted around these parts. It wasn't until I stopped by a local state forestry office and got directions from a ranger who also fly-fished that I was able to find my way onto one of the few unmarked public access points on the river.

The Brazos flowed swift and clear over a bed of bronze and golden cobblestones. The narrow stream was bordered by brushy willows and cottonwoods and afforded little room for back casts. It would be tricky, fast fishing. But I had the stream entirely to myself. I fished for a few hours in the cold, fast water and caught nothing. The river cobblestones were all shapes and irregular sizes and they were covered with a filmy green slime that was dangerously slick. Once I slipped on an algae-covered rock and fell painfully on my behind, shipping water into my hip boots. The icy sensation jolted my heart. The river was shallow but the current very strong, the mountain stream racing with water that not long ago had been snow on a mountain peak. Insect hatches weren't plentiful on these kinds of swift and narrow freestone streams. Trout wouldn't grow particularly large in this river—too little mayfly and caddis activity, not enough sustenance. But I had been advised by the forest ranger that a strategically placed dry fly could be a good bet. I waded upstream into knee-deep riffles, casting flies that floated on the surface, trying to keep my back casts high and my line out of the willows. I didn't see a single trout rise. And so I fished my way back downstream using sunken flies. It was a frustrating experience trying to hook these little river combatants that I couldn't even see. I was beginning to wonder if maybe the Brazos had been fished out. The bag limits on the river were very generous, which meant the river had to be constantly restocked with hatchery plantings.

I drove back to my campsite on the bank of the Chama River and fished that stream where it passed by the campground. The current flowed briskly, but with a little less speed than it did on the Brazos, and the pace was more to my liking. I was hoping for an evening hatch of mayflies to get the trout rising, but the insects and the trout had other plans. And so I retired for a second night without knowing how it felt to hook a New Mexican trout.

17

FROM THE FARAWAY NEARBY

As I DROVE south out of Chama, the green hills of New Mexico gave way once again to a red desert more characteristic of luminously lit landscape paintings. The New Mexican light was transparent. I would come to think of this dazzling brightness as "adobe light." It made me immediately visualize stretched canvases and the osseous shapes of sun-bleached bones floating over the desert. And I wondered, too, if in an alternate universe somewhere, cattle were constantly painting Georgia O'Keeffe's skull.

That flat-topped blue mesa in the distance looked familiar. Surely that was the Pedernal. This might have been my first visit to New Mexico, but I recognized that mountain instantly. Georgia O'Keeffe once said of the Pedernal: "It is my private mountain. . . . God told me if I painted it enough, I could have it."

She walked among these red hills. She put this land on canvas. The desert was filled with her light and spirit. The high desert town of Abiquiu, once an ancient pueblo, was famous as the place where Georgia O'Keeffe had lived during her most productive years. You couldn't visit her studio home except by special appointment; nor was there any museum of her paintings in the neighborhood. But you could walk her desert. Georgia O'Keeffe had found in the emptiness and space and light of this place, in its breathless stillness and exposure to the power of nature, a world reflecting her own creative thoughts. And she, in turn, added her character and fame to the region's own.

You couldn't barge in on the artist's adobe home in Abiquiu, but you could visit Ghost Ranch. Georgia O'Keeffe had lived and painted at Ghost Ranch when she first settled in New Mexico. The ranch was now the Ghost Ranch Living Museum, where wild animals were cared for that had been hurt or abandoned. They were returned to the wild when they were well enough to survive on their own. A geologic exhibit explained the evolution of nearby rock formations. By looking through the telescope, I could see millions of years exposed in the face of the cliffs. Visitors could walk interpretive trails that explained the area's natural and cultural history. On the grounds of the Ghost Ranch Conference Center, near the museum, a dinosaur dig was under way. Visitors were invited to inspect a small museum on local archaeology. But the real joy of Ghost Ranch was to walk the hiking trails among the red cliffs and grassy fields and gaze upon the vistas that inspired America's supreme painter of landscapes.

Just look at this land, I thought. The high desert was broken by vast irregular cliffs and soft hills of hot colors. At the top of the highest rocks were gray-green shales supported by thin bands of grayish gypsum. Below this layer was a flowing apron of pink sandstone cliff. These cliffs rested upon on a base of bloodred-and-chocolate piling. The hills and cliffs were streaked in rich iron oxides that brought out the hot red shades.

The cliffs immediately behind Ghost Ranch reflected heat

and color. In the transparent envelope of air, in a magnification of the far-off landscape, other hills and mesas appeared closer than they actually were. The flat top of the Pedernal stood smooth and perfect, as if poured from an hourglass. A blue sky presided serenely over the desert.

In her paintings, O'Keeffe smoothed away the sharpness and roughness to show the desert flowing in voluptuous and rapturous ways. She painted a land of great tenderness. Her hills grow soft and collapsing and pour like fluid. The radiant light of New Mexico shines on everything. She had the vision and talent to paint not the just the land she saw but the land she felt.

She turned landscapes into dreams. She did this by erasing the reality of the middle distance. By eliminating the middle ground that establishes the true scale of things, she brought the faraway and nearby together. Thus she was able to transform the recognizable into the mysterious. Her landscapes are clearly recognizable as the terrain of the American Southwest. And yet they are abstract, too, and this gives her work its heightened sense of reality. She even signed her letters "From the faraway nearby."

Her brush transformed cattle skulls and pelvic bones into her greatest icons. The bones seem a wholly natural part of the desert. She thought of the bones as symbols of a strong land. She denied the gleaming shapes represented death, but death is there, and also serenity and harmony and timelessness.

Georgia O'Keeffe defined a world of red hills, floating skulls, *penitente* crosses, and adobe churches, and her name grew to become a part of New Mexico. I wanted to linger here at Ghost Ranch; but I also wanted to move on to Santa Fe to see the new Georgia O'Keeffe Museum, which had opened the previous year. The new museum houses the world's largest permanent collection of her works. I wanted to stand in the physical presence of paintings that up until now I had only seen reproduced in photographs.

Continuing south along the highway, I spotted a sign calling my attention to the Hernandez Elementary School. I hit the brake, pulling over to the side of the road. Could this be the town of Hernandez? I checked my map. What a shock. I looked eastward across the highway for some sign, an adobe church, a simple cemetery with white crosses, anything. What I saw was a Southwestern version of a small but growing suburbia with untidy ranch houses and gas stations and the usual signs of highway culture.

On the last day of October, in 1941, Ansel Adams was driving on this very road, looking out at the empty hills of the Chama River Valley. He was heading toward Santa Fe, fifty miles away. In his autobiography, he described what happened next:

Driving south along the highway, I observed a fantastic scene as we approached the village of Hernandez. In the east, the moon was rising over distant clouds and snow-peaks, and in the west, the late afternoon sun glanced over a south-flowing cloud bank and blazed a brilliant white upon the crosses in the church cemetery. I steered the station wagon into the deep shoulder along the road and jumped out, scrambling to get my equipment together. . . . With the camera assembled and the image composed and focused, I could not find my Weston exposure meter! Behind me the sun was about to disappear behind the clouds, and I was desperate. I suddenly recalled that the luminance of the moon was 250 candles per square foot. I placed this value on Zone VII of the exposure scale; with the Wratten G (No. 15) deep yellow filter, the exposure was one second at $f/32$. I had no accurate reading of the shadow foreground values. After the first exposure I quickly reversed the 8×10 film holder to make a duplicate negative, for I instinctively knew I had visualized one of those very important images that seem prone to accident or physical defect, but as I pulled out the slide the sunlight left the crosses and the magical moment was gone forever.

I knew it was special when I released the shutter, but I never anticipated what its reception would be over the decades. *Moonrise, Hernandez, New Mexico* is my most well-known photograph. I have received more letters about this picture than any other I have made. . . .

During my first years of printing the *Moonrise* negative, I allowed some random clouds in the upper sky area to show, although I had visualized the sky in very deep values and almost cloudless. It was not until the 1970s that I achieved a print equal to the original visualization that I still vividly recall.*

I saw the final print Adams made of *Moonrise* when it was on exhibition with his other works in San Francisco. The New Mexican landscape stretches in ghostly bands of light and darkness. It is the most splendid, mysterious, and haunting photograph I have ever seen. It is the vision of a seer.

Ansel Adams once described the landscape he saw surrounding Ghost Ranch as a place where clocks had ceased to keep time. He described it as a world existing between what he called the macro and the micro.

*Ansel Adams, with Mary Street Alinder, *An Autobiography* (Boston: Little, Brown and Company, 1996), pp. 231–232.

It should surprise no one that Ansel Adams and Georgia O'Keeffe became great friends and collaborators. His photographs and her paintings render not the land that appears to the naked eye, but expressions of what the artists felt when they saw these landscapes—and, by extension, statements of what they felt about life itself. In a sense, these works are self-portraits.

Each artist had the ability to see beyond the mere surface beauty of a landscape and present us with its supernal reality. We recognize this quality the moment we cast our eyes on their work. This is indeed how it all feels and looks. O'Keeffe and Adams were that rarity—two truly great artists whose work continues to enjoy universal popularity. It wasn't simply their choice of subject matter (although finding a great theme in life can be half the battle). They gave us a vision of a mystical and sometimes fearful world that they knew was really out there, a world that forms the bedrock of our being. Between the macro and the micro. From the faraway nearby.

Cars and trucks barreled past me on the two-lane highway. There was nothing I could see before me, not in the prefab ranch houses and pseudo-adobe of present-day Hernandez, nor in the highway culture and beginnings of commercial sprawl, even to suggest that Ansel Adams had taken his famous photograph here. The contemporary world had finally caught up with Hernandez, New Mexico. I realized the clocks had finally started ticking. I got back into my car and drove on to Santa Fe.

18

SANTA FAKE

ANY CITY WITH more art galleries than bars is asking for trouble. At last count, Santa Fe had over 250 galleries, but you would have to look long and hard to find paintings that are disturbing or confrontational. Santa Fe is tourist Southwest. The town's appeal comes from its Spanish and Indian artwork and adobe architecture. It is a marvelous, affluent, and somewhat pretentious place. "Santa Fake," its detractors call it. This is the New Mexico out of which clichés are born: adobe houses with steer skulls mounted over doorways and dried red chile *ristras* hanging on porch walls. The air up here is thin and dry and the high desert causes Santa Fe to radiate light.

Santa Fe crowns a high-desert plateau, seven thousand feet above sea level, with mountain ranges visible all around. Its adobe architecture seems to grow out of the brown earth. The most prominent mountains are the Sangre de Cristos, which, when I rolled into town, were shining in the light of early afternoon, reflecting it back onto the adobe city. It is an incredible landscape, sun-drenched and luminous, with Indian pueblos lining the route from Santa Fe to Taos along the Rio Grande.

At this altitude, I couldn't imagine a more agreeable climate for a desert.

The western approach to Santa Fe on Cerrillos Road, however, came as a bit of a shock to me. Strip development and tourist tackiness had been plastered onto a timeless landscape, with a little pseudo-adobe architecture thrown in to relieve the eye. But there was still beauty and magic in the dirt roads winding up to the desert hills, and in the center of the town, old Santa Fe.

As late as the 1970s, most of the roads and streets in Santa Fe were still unpaved. Today, a house on a dirt road is a status symbol. Adobe mansions are going up in the piñon-dotted hills with a speed that astonishes and dismays many longtime Santa Feans. Everyone wants to live here, and property values reflect that fact. Tourists visit and can't get Santa Fe out of their heads. They want to bottle the magic and put it on a shelf, preferably a shelf in their own adobe homes. Adobe is nothing more than dirt, water, and straw, the cheapest building materials on earth, but today only the very wealthy can afford to buy an adobe house in Santa Fe. Maybe it is the high altitude and abundant sunshine or maybe it is the Spanish and Indian influences, but Santa Fe has a mystique.

Santa Fe depends on the romance of sunbaked adobe, even when the adobe is fake. The majority of modern "adobe" homes in Santa Fe are stucco. Real adobe homes, made from mud bricks and mud plaster, are thick all the way through, unlike the modern wooden-frame stuccos masquerading as adobes. Both kinds of adobe, the faux and the real, contribute to the so-called Santa Fe style. Homes and buildings appear smooth and rounded like the hills. On very old adobe homes, the bricks and mud contain bits of straw that make the brown structures take on a warm golden tone in certain kinds of light.

The walls on authentic adobe homes are thick, the doorways

recessed. Traditional adobes have only a few small windows. The low, flat-topped buildings call to mind Indian pueblos. Round wooden rafters known as vigas support the flat roofs. These vigas are usually made from pine timbers, and they are left exposed to view on the ceilings. Outside, they protrude through the walls for a foot or two, and people like to hang their chile *ristras* from them. Some adobe homes have enclosed patios that resemble small courtyards. Under moonlight, the adobe takes on a creamy, romantic light. The earthen structures suit the high-desert climate. Adobe resembles the desert itself. It is hard to tell where the earth ends and the adobe begins. More than anything else, adobe gives Santa Fe its feeling of timelessness.

Like every tourist, I wound up in the Plaza, the heart of Santa Fake. The Plaza is the soul of adobe land. Here are shops, restaurants, churches, museums, and galleries galore. The galleries are packed into the Plaza or on nearby Canyon Road, an artist's row. The Santa Fe Convention and Visitors Bureau boasts that visitors can find 1 million pieces of art within a single square mile. The bureau doesn't say how much of this coyote art is any good. Art isn't just confined to the galleries, either. I found it plastered all over town, on everything except the public urinals, as ubiquitous as the adobe architecture.

Flanking the northern side of the Plaza is the Palace of the Governors, a masterpiece of adobe design, and one of the oldest government buildings in the United States. Here is a trick question to ask at your next dinner party. See how many of your friends really know their American history. What is the oldest capital city in the United States? It is Santa Fe, of course, established in 1610, a decade before the Pilgrims landed at Plymouth Rock. The history of Europeans in the United States begins not with Englishmen settling Virginia and Massachusetts, as we were all led to believe as schoolchildren, but with the Spanish riding up out of Mexico. (And if you think of Indian pueblos as cities rather than small villages, then Acoma and Taos Pueblo vie with Old Oraibi on the Hopi mesa as the oldest continuously inhabited "cities" in the United States.)

Pueblo Indians lined the sidewalk in front of the Palace of the Governors, selling jewelry and pottery, exactly as Indians have been doing in Santa Fe for hundreds of years. The vendors were Zuni, Acoma, Tewa, and Rio Grande Indians. They sat beside their wares under the portal, the wide covered porch encircling the Palace, patiently answering dumb questions from tourists. The usual question was a variation on a theme of "How much is this?" Their handmade silver and turquoise jewelry and their exquisite pottery spread out on the blankets had all been fashioned by hand, and appeared to me to be truly outstanding examples of their art. The vendors are registered with the Palace of the Governors, which operates as a museum. Only the artists themselves or members of their immediate families are allowed to sell under the portal, thus guaranteeing the authenticity of all goods on display. I had been told that some of these artists earn upward of eighty thousand dollars a year. Not too shabby.

If the Indians ever get bored answering tourists' questions, they can always gaze across the grassy Plaza and take in the obelisk that commemorates the bravery of those who had "fallen in the various battles with savage Indians in the territory of New Mexico." Some years ago, there was a big stink in town over whether to get rid of the obelisk and its offensive inscription. One afternoon, a man simply climbed over the fence and chiseled out the word *savage,* thus ending the controversy. You can still see the gap in the plaque where the offending word was obliterated.

When the Rio Grande Indians rose up in the great Pueblo revolt of 1680 and drove the hated Spanish back into Mexico, they converted Santa Fe's Palace of the Governors into a pueblo. When the Spanish reconquered the Southwest twelve years later, those recapturing Santa Fe found a kiva in one of the palace's defensive towers. Today, the towers are gone; the shady portal was added in 1913.

I had to admit that the Plaza was as beautiful a public square as any I had ever seen. I found it ideal for watching people. Local citizens passed the time on benches, reading newspapers. A few were sprawled under the trees with a book. Young people tossed Frisbees and played Hacky Sack on the grass. Tourists flocked to the square for the ambience, a few no doubt asking themselves why their own charmless hometowns didn't have anything nearly this nice. The Plaza was in danger of being taken over entirely by tour groups. It was easy to understand why this square, shaded by blue pines, American elms, cottonwoods, and ornamental plum trees, is considered the essence of Santa Fe.

I began to look for the simple adobe building that houses the Georgia O'Keeffe Museum. I found the museum to be very much like her paintings—stark, simple, spare. I spent three hours touring the gallery, absorbed in such paintings as *Red Hills with Pedernal* and *Mule's Skull with Pink Poinsettia.*

Afterward, I poked into shops selling Indian pawn and pueblo pottery. I couldn't believe the prices. Behind the thick adobe walls of the Museum of New Mexico, I examined the remnants of Spanish colonial life: gowns, vestments, spurs, old wagon wheels known as *caretas,* and pine furniture that had been hewed by hand with adzes. Frankly, it all bored me stiff. I found those obligatory portraits of territorial administrators even less interesting. It was hard for me to believe that those arrogant men in the portraits had actually been flesh and blood.

Leaving the museum, I passed down narrow, winding streets lined with expensive shops and walled patios and shady courtyards. I found the famous Loretto Chapel, built for the Sisters of Loretto, the first nuns to come to New Mexico. The chapel contains a very famous wooden staircase, known as the Miraculous Staircase, which spirals upward in two complete 360-degree turns, without any central or visible support. It is said to have been built by an anonymous traveling carpenter who mysteriously arrived one day, as if in answer to the nuns' prayers. He built the miracle staircase and then disappeared like the Lone Ranger, without asking for thanks or payment. A good story and an apocryphal one. The nuns probably made it up to explain why they stiffed the carpenter.

I wanted to visit the author Richard Bradford, who makes his home in Santa Fe. Bradford had written an affecting coming-of-age novel back in the mid-sixties, *Red Sky at Morning*. I had liked the book very much. It was published to much popular and critical acclaim and, to the best of my knowledge, has never gone out of print. The novel tells the story of Josh Arnold, a seventeen-year-old boy forced to move to a hill town in New Mexico after his father, a shipbuilder in Mobile, Alabama, heeds the call to service in World War II. Bradford set his novel in a fictional New Mexican town he called Sagrado, a thinly disguised version of the old Santa Fe Bradford had known as a boy. There are also bits of Taos and Chimayó blended into the fictional town. Longtime Santa Feans often say that *Red Sky at Morning* gives the truest depiction of what Santa Fe had been like before it was discovered, when it was still a rustic, underpopulated, and uncomfortably remote mountain town.

American literature has a special form of the coming-of-age tale, featuring a city youngster maturing through experiences unique to the American West. In Jean Stafford's *The Mountain Lion*, a young girl's visit to a Colorado Ranch ends in death and high tragedy. In Edward Abbey's *Fire on the Mountain*, which the author based on true events, the twelve-year-old narrator, Billy Vogelin Starr, comes to the aid of his grandfather, a rancher who resists by force of arms all efforts by the federal government to seize his land for use as part of a missle-testing range. In Glendon Swarthout's *Bless the Beasts and Children*, an antiwar parable set within the painful cultural rift of the sixties, misfits at an Arizona boys' ranch attempt to save a buffalo herd targeted for slaughter by riflemen. Often these initiation tales fit into another literary category, which might be called "the stranger comes to town." In *Red Sky at Morning*, war and other circumstances force the novel's teenage narrator abruptly to take on the duties and responsibilities of adulthood while trying to come to terms with life in a tough but endearing New Mexican hill town.

I wanted to talk to Richard Bradford about what Santa Fe had been like back in those times when its streets were still packed with dirt. Above all, I wanted to ask him whether he thought his young hero, Josh Arnold, would find much if anything in present-day Santa Fe to test his mettle. I suspected Josh would have found the place a tourist trap and sorely in need of a little backbone.

Bradford's novel has a very powerful sense of place. He began writing it in the 1960s, while he was working as a publicist for the local tourist bureau, at a time when the Santa Fe he had known as a boy was beginning to change. His father, Roark Bradford, had been a well-regarded newspaperman in Atlanta and New Orleans. During the Depression, Roark Bradford bought a small house in Santa Fe, which the family used mostly on summer vacations. *Red Sky at Morning* recalls those times, presenting an affecting portrait of a remote New Mexican hill community as seen through the eyes of a wise adolescent. The novel explores the relationships between Anglos and Hispanics, and Josh, a witty, irreverent teenager, narrates his story with deadpan humor as he mingles with a cast of memorable and disarming local characters.

I began asking around town—at the public library and at the *Santa Fe New Mexican,* the daily newspaper—to see if anyone might be able to direct me to Bradford's house. A librarian told me she had heard Bradford was working over at St. Vincent's Hospital. I wound up over at the Santa Fe office of the *Albuquerque Journal North,* where I chanced upon that paper's editorial opinion writer, Anne Hillerman, Tony Hillerman's daughter, as it turned out. I caught her just as she was locking up the office at the close of day. She warned me Bradford might be a little sensitive about granting interviews. His creative output had dried up. (In an interview, Bradford had been quoted as saying that his muse had gone on vacation and was last seen in a San Pedro bar, picking up sailors.) *Red Sky at Morning* had been a best-seller. My copy of the Harper Perennial paperback proudly proclaimed on its cover that there were 1.5 million copies in print. Certainly nothing to be ashamed about there. But the author had trouble following up with a command performance. He published a pretty decent second novel, *So Far from Heaven* ("Poor New Mexico! So far from Heaven, so close to Texas," as the saying goes), and that was it.

I thought I was being the clever gumshoe, but I was only spinning my wheels. The author's whereabouts were no mystery—he was the Richard Bradford who was listed in the Santa Fe telephone directory as living on Harkins Lane. I then made an error worthy of a rookie journalist. I politely phoned the author with a request for an interview instead of ambling up to his doorstep and innocently introducing myself in person. One of the things I had learned while working as a newspaper reporter was that it's too easy to say no to a person over the telephone. Tougher when they have to look you in the eye. Richard Bradford answered his phone and said yes, he was the author of *Red Sky at Morning,* but no, he didn't care to meet with me. He said he had had some unhappy experiences in past interviews. I told him I wanted to talk about old Santa Fe. "I really don't think I have anything to say that could be helpful to you," he said politely but firmly.

Great. Perhaps John Ehrlichman, the Watergate conspirator, would be available to talk to me about the art of the novel. I was aware that he had come out here after serving his sentence for his Watergate crimes. Nixon's henchman had grown a beard and was said to have mellowed out. Ehrlichman settled down in Santa Fe to write fiction—political thrillers. He was supposed to be a pretty staunch environmentalist, too. Hell, everybody in Santa Fe seemed to be working on a novel or typing up a film treatment or doing something creative. Territorial governor Lew Wallace wrote part of *Ben-Hur* while he was officiating at the Palace of the Governors. Willa Cather finished *Death Comes for the Archbishop* while staying at the Santa Fe home of her friend Mary Austin, the pioneer conservationist and author. New Mexico had attracted more creative types than any other Southwestern state. Every third or fourth citizen in Santa Fe seemed to be painting a sunset or glazing clay pots or struggling over a word processor—that is when they weren't too busy repairing cracks in their adobe homes or discussing the water rights conveyed to their properties by right of the original Spanish land grants.

More than a thousand artists lived in town, a rather sobering statistic that came to me courtesy of the Santa Fe Convention and Visitors Bureau. (Santa Fe must register them like sex offenders.) New Age crystal-gazing vision questers were turning Santa Fe into a high-desert Lhasa. The town was ripe with swamis. Tibetan refugees lived in Santa Fe as part of a United States–Tibetan resettlement project. Santa Fe had more licensed acupuncturists than Beijing, or so it seemed. (One of those Santa

Fe acupuncturists, as it turned out, was my sister Elizabeth, a woman who once made her living as a hydrologist.) Opera singers, musicians, actors, and filmmakers all called Santa Fe home, even when home was a trophy house built high up in the hills and used mostly for vacations. Meanwhile, there were Ph.D.'s in town waiting on tables or driving taxicabs to meet the rent. Many Santa Feans had to give up and leave town, and increasingly many of those were Hispanic families whose roots in Santa Fe went back hundreds of years, all the way back to the original Spanish settlements.

I returned to the Plaza to watch the sun go down. The setting sun fired the flanks of the Sangre de Cristos—the Blood of Christ. Golden brown adobe radiated sundown tones and the old buildings subtly changed hue in the withdrawing light. There was a cantina not far from the Plaza, called the Pink Adobe, something of a landmark, and in the fading light I suddenly understood the reference. All around me adobe buildings and churches were turning pink, deepening into violet. The effect was nothing short of magical. No wonder so many people wanted to live here.

19

THE WAY TO TAOS

THE FOLLOWING MORNING found me on the High Road to Taos, the famous backcountry route that wends its way slowly up the foothills of the Sangre de Cristos. Each bend in the road added one more vista to my internal storehouse of beautiful places memorized. The pine-forested mountains rose up into a sky so blue, it appeared to be liquid. Willa Cather once wrote of this dome of delicious blue so close to the mountains: "Elsewhere the sky is the roof of the world; but here the earth was the floor of the sky."

Sleepy siesta villages came into view along the road. The highway led past orchards and adobe homes draped in bright red chile *ristras* hung out to dry under the sun. Brightly painted wooden crosses and *santos* appeared on adobe dwellings half-hidden behind piñons and juniper scrub. The turquoise trim on the houses had been put there to ward off the evil eye. Wooden crosses capped the sloping shoulders of an adobe church. Roadside stands sold *ristras* of dried red chile peppers and bottled honey and bread baked in *hornos*, outdoor adobe fireplaces shaped like beehives. There were roadside displays of *retablos* and *santos*, miniature carvings of Roman Catholic saints lovingly hand-carved and painted in vivid colors by local artists. Furniture that had been handmade with adzes, brightly-colored weavings, and embroidery were also on display. Many of these roadside tables went unmanned. If you wanted to purchase something, you simply walked up to the nearest house and knocked on the door.

The High Road led me to the ancient village of Chimayó and its famous Santuario. It was impossible to miss, what with the roadside signs marking the way to the tiny chapel. Chimayó is the Lourdes of the Southwest. Fortunately, it wasn't Holy Week, so at least there weren't ten thousand faithful lining the road, making the procession on foot, many of these pilgrims *penitentes* carrying wooden crosses on their backs. Parking was tough enough as it was. An astonishing number of people visit El Santuario de Nuestro Señor de Esquipas every year. Many are just curious tourists like myself, come to admire the architecture and religious art. Others come for the *milagros* and the curative power of the dirt. They scoop it up from a hole in the floor in the room off the main chapel, rubbing it over their afflicted parts. Or they shovel it into containers, to be carried home like take-out. It is a religion of candles, saints, and superstition, fatalism and suffering—not the American Catholicism I was raised on, but something almost pagan—Madonna worship and statues that sweat tears, and with images that appear like visions in the plaster. In the back room stands a shrine to the church's miracles, with canes, wheelchairs, crutches, and other medical paraphernalia hanging from the wall. I couldn't decide whether I liked the peasant art and brightly painted *santos* or if I thought it all kitschy trash. I did decide I liked the out-of-the-way little chapel called La Niña more than I liked the more popular Santuario. La Niña was deserted of tourists and my footsteps echoed eerily over its creaking wooden floor-boards.

Like most tiny New Mexican towns, Chimayó has grown up around its church. And like the church, the town attracts pilgrims, too—hungry people in search of what is widely considered to be the finest red chile pepper in New Mexico. Whatever was happening in the Santuario, I found that miracles really do come out of the dirt in Chimayó. Chile pepper is the true *milagro*. The best green chiles are said to be the Hatch chiles grown in southwestern New Mexico. But the best reds come from Chimayó. To speak frankly, I really hadn't had anything decent to eat on my trip until I arrived in New Mexico. There were a number of market stands near the Santuario selling "holy chiles," bags of ground dried chile pepper, red and green. I had a lot to choose from, but I was looking for one place in particular, the famous Leona's. Hers was a simple restaurant and shop. There were bags of green and red powder, along with bottled sauces and bagged tortillas. A small kitchen turned out tacos and burritos. I asked for a *carne adobado* burrito. I didn't care that it was only ten o'clock in the morning. I craved a taste of Leona's famous Chimayó chile.

Nowhere else does red chile attain such a depth of flavor. The *carne adobado*, pork marinated in a blend of red chiles, spread warmth throughout my mouth. Its flavors were rich and deeply soulful. This was unlike any Mexican food I had ever eaten. In traditional Mexican cooking—say the kind of cuisine that comes over the border from Chiapas or Sonora—the chiles act primarily as a condiment, a piquancy added to the more central flavors of meat and herbs and spices like cilantro, oregano, or cumin. This New Mexican cooking was a revelation. Here the earthen vegetable flavors of the chile pepper became the centerpiece, the deepest flavor of the dish. It was as if the meat filling acted merely as a conduit to the chile. I found the flavors brilliant and mouth-filling. The red Chimayó chile had a distinctly roasted, smoky flavor. A wine snob—say a writer for *Wine Spectator*—might say that he detected a rich pluminess with underlying hints of chocolate and spice. I tasted a second dish, an enchilada smothered in a fresh green chile sauce. Green chiles can be either hotter or milder than the reds—it all depends on the levels of capsaicin, a natural alkaloid in the pod that gives chile its fire. Reds come from dried chiles that have been allowed to ripen fully on the vine; green chiles are picked early. In the days before refrigeration and freeze-drying, New Mexicans enjoyed their green chile stews in the summertime and feasted on red chile dishes throughout the winter months. Nowadays, one can enjoy both green and red year-round. My sister Susan, who teaches elementary school and keeps llamas as pets, and lives in the rural community of Bosque Farms, south of Albuquerque, told me that her favorite time of the year is autumn, when the air of her valley takes on the sharp tang of peppers roasting over open fires. Harvest is over, the cottonwoods have turned lemon and gold, and families are putting up their peppers for the winter. In autumn, a favorite spectacle is to watch chile peppers being roasted by the bushel in rotating steel-mesh drums heated by hissing propane jets.

The fire in my green-chile enchilada snuck up on me more as an afterglow. I found the actual flavor of the green fruit to be more subtle and complex than the flavors created by the dried red powders. In New Mexico, most green-chile dishes are made almost exclusively from Hatch chiles. Hatch chiles are the identical cultivar as the Anaheims available in California markets. But the New Mexican peppers I tasted were hotter and more flavorful than those grown under California's milder climatic conditions. Cooler summer nights in the New Mexican high country raise the level of capsaicin. As for Chimayó chiles, one can add extra pods to a dish to deepen the flavor without increasing the heat. Caribe chiles turn up the heat; anchos add a rich smokiness. Both the green and red chiles I tasted at Leona's had overtones and undertones of rich, sensual flavors that seemed to grow above and around and under one another. The chile left a lingering afterglow in my mouth.

Philosophers asks, Why is there something rather than nothing? Why does anything exist at all? In New Mexico, the big philosophical question is "Red or green?" It is asked wherever chile is served. If you aren't sure which you like best, ask for "Christmas." You'll get both.

Flavor and heat vary from chile to chile, although the greens I tasted tended to be hottest. Chile can be used as an ingredient, or in a sauce, or as the central vegetable in a hearty stew. It is a staple of Southwestern cooking, as essential as corn and pinto beans. New Mexicans like to slather red and green sauces on such traditional Mexican fare as enchiladas, burritos, tamales, chiles rellenos, and huevos rancheros. The New Mexican versions of these dishes tasted far more more interesting than the Mexican versions I was familiar with, because chile was the central focus. Chile is an *essence,* investing a dish with earthy tones and brawniness. A pod or two thrown in the pot give a stew a special roasted warmth and deepness. New Mexicans put green chiles in omelettes and on top of steaks, as well as stuffing them into delicious warm pillows of airy bread called sopaipillas. An ordinary cheeseburger can be transformed into the miracle known as a green-chile cheeseburger. And native chefs have come up with the fire-breathing New Mexican specialty *carne adobado,* pork that has turned red from its long, long marinade in a sauce of chile pods and is then roasted along with the sauce.

Leona sold clear plastic bags of red and green chile powder and caribe, which are crushed chiles with their seeds. She had

188 · MICHAEL CHECCHIO

many glass jars of red and green chile sauces and salsas available. Her *ristras* came in one-, two-, and three-foot lengths. You could purchase dry mixes for cooking your own green and red chile stews, and mixes for baking green-chile corn bread and chipotle corn bread (chipotles are smoked peppers). You could stock up on such staples as dried sweet corn, *pozole*, which is white-corn hominy served as a side dish with most New Mexican meals, and *atole*, blue cornmeal. I counted assorted packages of fresh tortillas that had been baked that morning in her small factory just down the road from the restaurant. Leona had desserts, too: *bizcochito*, the official cookie of New Mexico, or so the tag on the bag said, fresh banana bread, and *panocha*, Leona's version of the traditional Lenten pudding. You could improve your mind with her book *Leona's Sanctuary: Her Recipes and Story* or take away an inspirational video, *The Shrine: The Story of El Santuario and Its Healing Dirt.*

I continued on my way, the warmth of the chiles spreading through my insides. The trees were dappled in sunlight and shade. The road climbed higher into pine-mantled mountains. From an overlook, I had a splendid view of the postcard village of Truchas under the snowcapped Sangre de Cristos. Robert Redford filmed *The Milagro Beanfield War* in this valley and the movie brought tourism to Truchas. Redford had come here for the clarity of the mountain light. Looking west, I could see all the way across the Rio Grande Valley to the Jemez Mountains and even make out the flat top of the Pedernal. The High Road continued on to Las Trampas, where there was a local church of some renown, a restored mission, its adobe parapets crowned with wooden pyramids and crosses. In time, the High Road got me to Taos.

TAOS IS LIKE a movie set for a Zen Western, an artistic haven for outdoor adventurists, New Age crystal gazers, and refugees from the hippie communes of the sixties. Artists, rich Californians, trust funders, aging flower children, cutthroat drug dealers, and poor Chicano sheepherders all call themselves Taoseños.

Fields of blue-green sagebrush surround the highway leading into town. Acres and acres of the lush plant roll outward toward Taos Mountain. The sagebrush on the flats of Carson Mesa seemed to change color with more regularity than the ocean.

Taos has been an art colony for a century. On a September day in 1898, the painters Ernest Blumenschein and Bert Phillips, on a sketching expedition, stopped in Taos to repair a busted wagon wheel. Their delay turned into an extended painting holiday. Blumenschein was so enchanted with the locale that he returned with his family every summer until 1918, when they took up residence permanently. Other artists followed, in pursuit of the adobe light and mystical mountains.

In 1918 Mabel Dodge, a busybody New York socialite, arrived in Taos with the intention of starting her own salon of writers and artists. Mabel, who was herself largely untalented, married for purposes of local color a Tewa Pueblo Indian named Tony Luhan, one of several husbands she collected over the years, and built a large and comfortable house for herself in Taos. Soon a succession of visionaries began showing up at the door of the gossipy patroness. There were the novelists D. H. Lawrence, Oliver La Farge, and Aldous Huxley, the choreographer Martha Graham, psychiatrist Carl Jung, the poet Witter Bynner, and Ansel Adams and Georgia O'Keeffe, to name the major luminaries. The author of *Lady Chatterley's Lover*, famously prudish in real life, was so shocked by the lack of privacy in Mabel's home that he painted her bathroom windows black. Lawrence had tuberculosis and came to New Mexico for the dry air. He died in France, the disease having turned his lungs into cheesecloth by the end, but his ashes were buried at Kiowa Ranch, fifteen miles north of Taos. Mabel Dodge Luhan must have carried a torch for Lawrence, for she tried to make a gift of the ranch to the author, but Lawrence refused, wisely not wanting to be in her debt. His wife, Frieda, later accepted the ranch in exchange for the original manuscript of *Sons and Lovers*. But Frieda was so afraid Mabel would steal the author's ashes that she mixed the mortal remains of D. H. into the cement of a small shrine that she had fashioned into the shape of a cabin.

The counterculture and the hippies followed the artists into Taos. Film director Dennis Hopper showed up to film scenes at a Taos hippie commune for his landmark movie, *Easy Rider*. Hopper went on to buy the old Mabel Dodge Luhan House and spend his wild-man drug years in Taos.

As you drive up from the south, Highway 68 transforms itself into Paseo del Pueblo Sur, a cheesy and blighted strip of budget motels, gas stations, and fast-food emporiums. The asphalt strip changes its name briefly to Santa Fe Road before being reborn as Paseo del Pueblo Norte. I got stuck in a permanent bottleneck that seems to exist in the center of town, where Highway 68 and US 64 meet up only a block away from the famous Plaza. Everything grinds to a halt at this intersection; this traffic jam seems to be a way of life in Taos. From what I could see of it, the heart of Taos seemed given over almost exclusively to tourism. But at least they had tried to make the old part look good. As in Santa Fe, nothing in the old town stands over two stories. I walked around the Plaza's portal, stepping into curio shops and checking out silver concha belts and turquoise jewelry. Later, I drove up to Taos Pueblo to see the old adobe dwellings. Among many contributions to our culture, I guess you could say American Indians invented apartment dwelling. Taos Pueblo is the largest and most architecturally ambitious of America's surviving pueblos. The Indians no longer reside there but live in modern homes nearby on the reservations. As at other reservations, I sensed the Indians both welcomed and resented visitors. I felt almost saddened and discouraged walking around the ancient complex. I couldn't help but notice the interesting fee arrangements: five dollars to park, five dollars to possess a still camera, ten dollars to point a video camcorder at the pueblo, a fifteen-dollar fee to sketch it, and thirty-five dollars to capture it in watercolors or oils. The last is possibly in revenge for all the bad coyote art that has come out of the Southwest.

I stopped in Brodsky's Bookstore on Paseo del Pueblo Norte near the Plaza and asked one of the owners, Rick Smith, if he knew how I could get in touch with the novelist John Nichols, who lives in Taos. Earlier, I had written a letter to Nichols requesting an interview. I had sent it in care of one of his publishers, Henry Holt, and knowing that Nichols likes to fly-fish for trout, I had also sent along a copy of a collection of fly-fishing essays that I had published. Nichols's memoir, *The Last Beautiful Days of Autumn,* has many magical fly-fishing scenes set in the Rio Grande Gorge. I hadn't heard back from Nichols—it turned out that Henry Holt hadn't forwarded my letter and book because the publishing house didn't have his address, which made me wonder how they managed to get the author's royalties to him. Smith said he would call Nichols for me, but he warned I might have to wait a few hours, as the author slept in during the day and didn't awaken until midafternoon.

It turned out that Nichols said he would be pleased to see me. We met at a café near the bookstore. John ordered a late-afternoon breakfast of potatoes and fried eggs. He told me he was a night person, writing all night, usually in longhand, and then turning in at dawn. One hand was conspicuously swathed in bandages. Writer's cramp? I asked him.

"A dog tried to get my cat," Nichols explained.

"Looks like the dog won."

"Well, the cat's all right, anyway."

I had intended to question Nichols about magical realism and the New Mexico novel, but mostly we ended up talking about trout fishing. We both agreed it was as good an excuse as any to stand in a pretty place all day. Nichols said he liked fishing a fly sunk deep in fast water, the kind of rough water found in the hard-to-reach recesses of the Rio Grande Gorge. I told him I looked forward to fishing the Rio Grande and explained to him my lack of success on other New Mexico streams. We both spoke about the visual and tactile pleasures of trout fishing. "I love to feel that tug on the line," John said. "I never get bored with it." Nichols mentioned to me that he was suffering from Ménière's disease, a malfunctioning of the semicircular canal of the inner ear, the same affliction that had once grounded the astronaut Alan Shepard. It was increasing in its severity, causing John to lose his balance more frequently, but he wasn't letting it keep him from fly-fishing. Despite his condition, he looked lean and incredibly fit and far younger than his fifty-eight years. Maybe that says something about the outdoor life in Taos.

By the time he came to Taos, in 1969, Nichols had already written two critically acclaimed novels, *The Sterile Cuckoo* and *The Wizard of Loneliness.* An easterner, he had spent the summer of his sixteenth year in New Mexico, had seen Taos, and had never forgotten the landscape or its effect on him. He used his modest payment for the film rights to *The Sterile Cuckoo* to purchase and renovate a small ramshackle adobe on a few acres of property at Ranchitos, not far from the narrow, brush-banked Pueblo River. Many of John's neighbors were Spanish-speaking subsistence farmers or sheepherders. Nichols and his wife arrived in the wake of the hippie invasion of Taos and tensions were running high in the valley. The Spanish-speaking residents of Taos saw the hippies as a threat to their traditional rural way of life. The hippies, on the other hand, were rejecting the very middle-class values to which the Hispanics were aspiring. The air was thick with misunderstanding. The author had been involved in radical politics and the antiwar movement back in New York City. If he had come to Taos looking for some kind of refuge, he found instead a place to take a stand. In Taos, he encountered the same damaged American society and many of the same problems he'd met with back in Manhattan. But as he wrote in another memoir, *If Mountains Die,* the noise level in Taos was not quite so deafening.

By day, Nichols involved himself in the struggles of Taos Valley's poor Hispanic citizens, whose homes and rural way of life were under threat to development and complicated land swindles. At night, he labored over novels that publishers wouldn't buy. And then in 1972, in five weeks, Nichols, writing in longhand, produced the first draft of his comic masterpiece, *The Milagro Beanfield War.* It was to be the first in a series of chunky novels that would eventually become known as the *New Mexico Trilogy* (even though not a single reference to New Mexico appears in the text).

"I wrote that book very quickly," Nichols told me. "I had a first draft in five weeks. It took me three weeks to rewrite and correct it, and then three weeks to type it all up. I think I started writing the book in November 1972 and I think it was accepted in February 1973. And then I was given eight or ten months to rewrite it. And I did rewrite it a couple of times."

"I'm staggered that anyone could write a six-hundred-page novel in only five weeks," I said.

"I can always write the first drafts in one, two, three months. But then I have to rewrite for years. Sixty percent of the time my books never get published anyway."

The Milagro Beanfield War is a book full of love, humor, and a healthy outrage. Nichols brought to life a sleepy fictional village very much like the Hispanic settlements where he lived. His novel told the story of hardscrabble villagers living close to the land who rose up and rebelled in their own hilarious fashion against a rich gringo developer. It was inspired by those Taoseños Nichols knew who were guardians of their beautiful valley. And it is nothing less than the human comedy, the kind of novel Nichols loves to write, a book filled with a huge cast of characters and a panoramic overview. The publisher pleaded with the author to change the obscure title, but Nichols stood his ground. *The Milagro Beanfield War* became a kind of classic. Readers were immediately reminded of the humanity of John Steinbeck and the magical realism of Gabriel García Márquez, but the book is uniquely Nichols.

"I had been living in Taos for three years when I wrote that book," Nichols said. "I had been involved in many community conflicts and struggles, including working with the Tres Rios Association, trying to block the building of a large dam. During that time, I also wrote for a muckraking journal, *The New Mexico Review*, and many of my articles were about land and water rights and conflicts. I was also heavily involved with my community's irrigation activities. So there were lots of discussions about land, water, and community politics."

John was much taken with Taos, the kind of place where one can walk down the street and easily get into political and literary discussions with friends and neighbors. The author had gone on to write several nonfiction books about his life there. My personal favorite was *The Last Beautiful Days of Autumn*, the author's memoir of the simple pleasures and hardships of living in the northern New Mexico high country. Nichols would describe routines and daily pleasures that wore well: a hike up to Tres Orejes Mountain with an old friend; the discovery of a blowhole full of rattlers; the last firewood run before snow flurries swept down the valley and autumn died in a glorious whiteout. And of course there was the trout fishing in the Rio Grande Gorge, where the trails have forbidding names like Little Arsenic and Suicide Slide.

That book is illustrated by haunting photographs that John had taken himself of Carson Mesa, Taos Mountain, and the surrounding countryside near his home. You can feel the power emanating from the landscape in those photographs. My favorite was a moody winter shot of the snow-covered Rio Grande Gorge at dusk, taken from the center of the bridge span, the lens capturing the lonely scene. John told me he taught photography workshops in town.

I asked him what he was working on at the present time. He said his most recent novels had been rejected for publication. There was nothing new about that, he said, his work having been frequently rejected over the course of his career. "I don't write good books," he joked.

"I'm writing a novel that I've been working on since 1988," he said. "The first drafts are over a thousand pages. I'm sure I wrote that first draft in just under four months. By and large, that's the speed I turn out a draft. I pretty much wrote the initial draft in longhand. Then I like to transpose my drafts onto a computer. By the way, I like to write in the bathtub. I write and correct manuscripts there."

I asked the novelist about some of the changes he's seen in Taos over the years. I wanted to know if the old Hispanic families he encountered when he had first moved to Taos were still in the valley, or whether middle-class development and rising property values had driven them out.

"You have to understand that when I first came to this town," John said, "many of my neighbors and those friends I made were between sixty and eighty years old. Most of those

196 · MICHAEL CHECCHIO

families are still here, but the older generation, the elderly people, died. Their children are still around, but fewer of them are involved in agricultural pursuits.

"We still have all the same issues that have been around for the last thirty years. The adjudication of water. Too many people living in too small a place. An overabundance of rafters on the Rio Grande. Too many rich people wanting the community's services, but without a tax base. There's a lot of development here, as there is anywhere else. People sell their land, bit by bit, piece by piece. These are all problems.

"One of the real detrimental effects we've seen recently in the development of Taos comes from people who are building secondary, recreational homes. These people choose to live here part-time but don't really participate or contribute to the community, and that has an alienating effect. They take up land and space without being contributing members of the town, and that will always hurt any kind of a community.

"Taos County is very poor. Thirty-five or forty percent of the county is living below the poverty level. New Mexico is the poorest state in the union, officially. A majority of the people around here work for wages that are a couple of bucks within the minimum wage.

"But that's the neat thing about Taos. The longtime indigent people hang tough. It's really hard to get them out. There are a great many people in this county who own houses but can't get jobs, and it's difficult to survive. But they hustle and shuffle, and consequently, sixty-two percent of the county is still Chicano. Seventy-five percent of the kids in the schools are Hispanics."

Nichols is a die-hard conservationist, but he isn't bitter about the changes in Taos. "You can't go anywhere on the globe and not find development changing the face of a place. I don't think there's anything unusual about Taos. There's no place that's not going to get bigger," he said.

I asked John about the introduction he had written for W. L. Rusho's biography, *Everett Ruess: A Vagabond for Beauty*. Thinking about the doomed teenager drawn to the Southwest, Nichols had been reminded of the famous concluding passage in F. Scott Fitzgerald's *The Great Gatsby*, where the Jazz Age author describes an American continent still green and uncharted at the dawn of its discovery by Europeans, a continent presenting humanity for the last time in history with a place still commensurate to its capacity for wonder. Mankind was losing that capacity, Nichols wrote in his introduction to the Ruess biography. He warned that we need to restore that capacity for wonder in order to survive, need to learn to relove the natural world that we are busy dismantling. I asked John whether he thought that the American West was one of those few places left to us where one could regain that original capacity for wonder—a true last, best place.

"No, you can do it anywhere you live," Nichols said. "You can do it in New York City."

And of course, Nichols is right. Navajo Mountain over in Utah may be the sacred mountain of the Dineh, but the sacred mountain is everywhere. By moving into and inhabiting a landscape, wherever that landscape is, we discover the sanctity of the earth, and this recognition allows us to try to match our own nature with the land's power and beauty. Carson Mesa is everywhere. Taos Mountain is everywhere. The Milagro Beanfield is all around us.

LATER THAT EVENING, after my meeting with John Nichols, I wound up having dinner at a remarkable joint in Taos called Fred's Place, on Paseo del Pueblo Sur. Fred's Place turned out to be a real find. It is probably the most popular restaurant in Taos, not because it is in any way chic or trendy but because the food is so good. When I arrived, I was told there would be an hour's wait. But a lady dining with a small child invited me to her table.

Her name was Rose Ortiz and the child was her grand-daughter, Melinda. Born in Santa Fe and raised in Albuquerque, Rose had been living in Taos for the past twenty-six years. Her family was descended from Spanish land-grant heirs. Her great-aunt used to own a home on fifteen acres in Santa Fe in the Montoya Hill district, but her aunt's son, who inherited the house, and who "wasn't all there" mentally, Rose explained, failed to pay taxes and the authorities auctioned off the property without the family's knowledge.

"No one bothered to inform us," Rose told me. "We only found out later that the house and the fifteen acres were sold for the back taxes."

"Who bought it?" I asked

"John Ehrlichman," she said.

Now that was interesting. "The John Ehrlichman of Watergate fame?" I asked.

"Right, the Watergate guy," Rose said. "It was a low blow. I wasn't crazy about it, I can tell you, what with his being a convicted crook and all. No one even bothered to inform my mom. You know how families are—they become separated after a while. My mom probably would have bought the house and the property had she known about this."

My waiter arrived with an order of tamales. I had asked for my meal "Christmas style." Half the tamales covered in green sauce, the other in red, with the obligatory *pozole* on the side. Rose and her granddaughter had already finished their dinner. I sampled a forkful of the red-sauced tamale.

"I tasted this same red chile earlier today," I told Rose. "This chile comes from Chimayó, doesn't it? I can actually taste the difference in the chiles." Rose said Chimayó chile has a quality all its own. She told me that the restaurant owner, Fred, an Anglo, had gotten many of the recipes by talking to old-time Hispanic families in the area and then carefully writing it all down. I sampled the green sauce. It was amazing—subtler and more complex than the red. I decided I liked it best.

Rose told me she came to Taos with the hippies in 1970. Her husband, Cecil, an Anglo, had been a student at the University of New Mexico at the time. He used to travel up to the Taos Valley to fish for trout in the Rio Grande. There was an old Hispanic couple living in the town of Questa, just north of Taos, who supplemented their income by selling earthworms and other live bait to fishermen like Cecil. Rose and her husband got to know the elderly couple, who mentioned to them that they were thinking of selling their old adobe house. The old folks were tired of having only cold running water and having to heat the place with firewood. But to Rose and Cecil, the 150-year old adobe was a dream come true. They bought the house and five and three-quarter acres of land for twelve thousand dollars.

"We wanted to get away from all the hubbub of society, and Taos seemed like the perfect place for that," Rose said. "It was a gorgeous, cute little old house. There was this old wood-burning stove. We had running water—cold water only. There was just a bathtub, and you had to heat the water for it. We did a lot of renovating. It was wonderful in those days."

I asked Rose if she ever felt out of place in Taos. Tensions were very high in those days and fights were breaking out between hippies and young Hispanics who resented and feared the presence of the newcomers. It was a cultural clash. And Rose had a foot in both worlds.

"Well, I guess my husband and I were considered hippies. But we had bought a place—we weren't camping or squatting on anybody's property. We weren't living on any of the communes, like the Hog Farm. So we weren't looked at as being grubby hippies. Our intention was to stay and live here."

It took awhile for Rose and her husband to fit in. But their acceptance grew as they became involved in the community. Rose was active on the school board and became a dental assistant at a clinic in Questa.

"Even though I spoke Spanish, the old folks didn't take to me for a couple of years. But once they got to know us, most of the folks really started to care for us and accept us into their culture. Even the *brozs*—you know, the younger kids, the ones the hippies were having the real trouble with—even they began to accept us. And remember, it wasn't the old folks who snubbed us; it was the younger generation who didn't care for hippies. I never really got harassed, but then I spoke Spanish, too, so that always helped. The hippies who stayed and became a part of the community started to get along with the old Spanish families, and after a while even the younger generation of Hispanics, for the most part, didn't bother them anymore. You know the ones I'm talking about—the *brozs?* That's what we called the uneducated types, sort of like LA *chollas* or lowriders. Well, everybody became a little more open-minded. We began to party together and have really good times, and things were really copacetic."

For the first fifteen years, Rose didn't really notice many big changes occurring in Taos. "It was always hard to make any kind of a living out here without working two or three jobs. Unless you had some type of a career. Fortunately, I got trained as a dental assistant at the Questa Clinic. So I was accepted more easily."

In 1980, the molybdenum mine in Questa shut down and property values around Taos temporarily went into a slump, along with the economy. Rose, who by this time had broken up with her husband, was able to buy a house in the old historic section of Taos for about fifty thousand dollars. She reckons the value of her property has tripled since that time, as has the value of the old adobe house in Questa, which her exhusband still owns and which their daughter Rhonda will one day inherit. Rose told me her daughter held down two jobs and still couldn't make ends meet. "That's why she's living back home here with mom," Rose said.

Rose told me that Taos had a huge art scene, "but only a handful of really successful artists—guys like R. C. Gorman—are making a living at it. It takes every dime they can earn just to make ends meet out here."

Squabbles continued to break out over old land grants. The Taos Indians were still fighting to restore lands that were taken from them by the federal government. Many of the Spanish-speaking subsistence farmers had left the Arroyo Seco area. Homes for millionaires were going up in place of patch farms and subsistence gardens. The actress Julia Roberts had moved to Taos a few years back and bought up acreage near Des Mondes.

"Farming is basically dying out," Rose told me. "The old folks can't afford the taxes and the kids have moved away to make a living, and no one's there to take over the ranching and farming."

The computer age has allowed people to move to Taos "by the gross," Rose said. She had a friend, a Texas oil man, who "commuted" to work in the Lone Star State by modem. But Rose doubted that Taos would ever expand to become as large as Santa Fe. There is no airport to land a Learjet in the Taos Valley. "Everybody in town is opposed to building an airport," Rose told me. "I mean, everybody is pretty much agreed on that—no one wants this to become another Aspen." Taos is strict about ordinances and growth limits, she said. And a lot of the open land outside of Taos is protected as BLM and Forest Service timberlands and Indian tribal grounds.

"Let me tell you what's so beautiful about Taos," Rose said. "Twelve years ago, I had a bout with breast cancer. The disease was in a very aggressive stage. If I'd still been living back in Albuquerque, where I was raised, I probably would have been just one more person who got sick. I doubt I would have gotten any other people except my immediate family to come to my aid and help me out. But when I got sick, people from Taos and Questa and Red River, all my friends, gathered around to help." Rose said her friends raised money to take care of bills that her insurance wouldn't cover, and that raised her spirits and helped her rally. "These are the kinds of things that make Taos so special," she said.

"I only hope that people can learn to appreciate what Taos is really all about. Taos is one of the most spiritual places I've ever seen. Maybe it's the Indian and Spanish and hippie influences, but they're all very spiritual people out here. I hope people can understand this. People out here are open and in tune. Everyone should try to live at this level. That's what's so beautiful about Taos. People around here are so grateful to be alive and to be out here and they really take the time to appreciate it."

Outside, it was darkening. The sun had set low over Carson Mesa, leaving a thin band of lemon and coral on the edge of the sky. The flow of earthly day was vanishing into a rich blue night. Lights came on in the valley under the solid blackness of Taos Mountain. A dark magic emanated from the earth. I thought of the words of Mabel Dodge Luhan, who wrote a memoir of her life in Taos. She, too, had gazed upon Taos Mountain in the deep wine of twilight. And her words echoed what generations of Taoseños have felt about their mountain. I looked at its dark mysterious shape and I felt it, too. "It seemed to me the mountain was alive," Mabel wrote, "awake and breathing. That it had its own consciousness. That it knew things. . . . The mountain seemed to smile and breathe forth an infinitely peaceful, benevolent blessing as the light faded away from it."

20

MAGICAL REALISM

EARLY NEXT MORNING, I drove eastward up into the Sangre de Cristo Mountains, crossing the Continental Divide. For the first time since my trip had begun, rivers began to drain east. Tall ponderosa pines lined the steep banks where the Cimarron River poured out of a narrow canyon below Eagle Nest Lake. Eastward lay the high plains, those grasslands stretching into infinity, where an altogether different kind of West began. I was coming to the end of my journey.

Cimarrón is a Spanish word, and it means "untamed." Meteorologists are always going on about how the town of Cimarron, at the eastern base of the Sangre de Cristos, gets blasted by more thunderstorms than any other spot in the country. I suspect the townspeople are secretly proud of that fact. Cimarron was once a Wild West town. Twenty-six men were murdered inside the historic Saint James Hotel alone. I don't know how many died outside on the streets. Jesse James, Wyatt Earp, Doc Holliday, Billy the Kid—everyone who was anyone in the gunfighter world all passed through Cimarron.

When I was in Cimarron, I wondered if any of the tourists

visiting the outlaw sites and pointing their camcorders were experiencing moments of cognitive dissonance right then. A massive manhunt was still under way on the other side of New Mexico for the fugitive sociopaths who had closed down vacation sites like Grand Gulch and Hovenweep. The gunsels hadn't been caught yet. I doubted any tourist who chanced upon them would think the experience called for a Kodak moment. Nothing romantic about those fellows at all. I wondered if the tourists posing for snapshots in front of the St. James Hotel would think it colorful if the killers were to come out to Cimarron and start shooting up the nearby Philmont Boy Scout Ranch. Perhaps a century from now, after enough time has passed between the reality and the act, the places these modern-day fugitives passed through while on the lam will become tourist attractions in their own right. But I was interested in trout, not outlaws; in the Cimarron River, not the town.

So I drove back up to the canyon in the pines. The Cimarron River was a little too close to the road for my taste. But I saw few anglers bothering the stream. I found a roadside pullout and parked. In the canyon, I could plainly hear the sound of water, rushing water. The scene was beautiful: sunlight, tree shade, a gurgling river. The kind of moment I knew only death would obliterate.

I waded upstream, trying to lose myself in the rhythm of the casting. I fished with a dry fly, laying it on the water as delicately as I could. It was tricky because the river was narrow and brushy and the casting tough. Tree branches snagged my fly on the back cast. The Cimarron River was little more than a narrow and intimate creek, by my standards. Not my ideal trout stream—too narrow and brushy, too close to the road. But the canyon was very scenic, no denying that. The rock facade known as the Palisades rose impressively above the pines.

The river drew the light upon it and seemed to reveal something deeply significant about being, existing. I was much taken with the river's ability to attract light, its power to receive it. Standing in the river, I felt a very agreeable sensation being conferred upon me. The river seemed to be particles of light, a moment-to-moment flow of phenomenal experience.

In time, I became engaged in the fishing, so that I was no longer absorbed in the scenery. This was a state of concentration fly fishermen sometimes get into, where one is barely aware of anything except the water within casting range. It was as if the world had telescoped down into the moment. I no longer had a conscious awareness of the visual beauty of the canyon. No thoughts, simply the sensation of the situation, as an animal experiences reality.

But the fountain I was standing in changed. I was conscious that I wasn't catching any trout. I kept looking for glints of trout in the riffles, for shadows near the rocks. I began to wonder if the river was fished out. I blamed the road, so close to the river. I blamed the lack of good fishing regulations and the overly generous creel limits. But most of all, I was beginning to doubt my abilities. I had yet to catch a New Mexican trout. I was fishing in one of the most agreeable landscapes on earth and I was getting discouraged.

I changed flies, switching from dries to wets and back again. Nothing helped. I fished all levels of the shallow stream. I overturned wet rocks and examined them for mayfly and caddis husks, to see if I was using the right kinds of flies. In my mind, I imagined a trout floating up directly under my fly, the moment prolonged in excitement, then the sudden take and lightning twitch. But that delicious moment never came.

Fly-fishing is about mystery. If it were easy, it would soon lose much of its appeal. Anglers try to peer behind the masks of water. It is a foreign and mysterious environment. A body of water is a mirror when first looked into. Its surface reveals little; it reflects what is above it. If it is a river, it is moving and shimmering, always changing, while always appearing to remain in place. They say mountains are old but that rivers are new, remaking themselves moment by moment. You can watch a river for hours and never become bored. Water fascinates us, and the best water, to my thinking, conceals trout.

You have to learn how to look at trout water, how to read and study it. Trout will reveal themselves as a shadow on the bottom, or a dimple rising on the surface. We call fly-fishing an art and a science, although it is only a pastime. But this metaphorical approach is the romance of fly-fishing. And no matter how expert a fly fisherman one becomes, there will always be something a little mysterious about the experience. The mysterious, Einstein once told us, is the fundamental emotion that stands at the cradle of true art and true science. We require mysteries more than we need solutions.

FROM CIMARRON I drove back to Taos. And from Taos back to Santa Fe. This time, I took the Low Road, passing by the white-water runs of the Taos Box under steep-sided cliffs lining the Rio Grande. And the next day on to Albuquerque, a two-hour drive.

You could see a distant pallor. A haze of pollution hung over the sprawling city, visible miles away. The Sandia Mountains rose five thousand feet at the eastern edge of Albuquerque. A few months earlier, as I was getting ready for my trip to the Southwest, I had rented a video copy of the film *Lonely Are the Brave*. Kirk Douglas has always considered this his favorite among his many films. It is based on Edward Abbey's novel *The Brave Cowboy*. The novel, and the film made from it, concern the passing of the traditional American West. Abbey told the story of Jack Burns, a contemporary cowboy fighting civilization, trapped in a mid-century America that is cutting him off from the only life he has ever known or wanted. The film version, shot in crystal-clear black and white, came out in 1962. The movie concludes with a chase filmed atop Sandia Peak above Albuquerque, with Jack Burns running from the law. The town in the film appears no bigger than a truck stop. The Sandias in the movie are untamed, covered entirely in juniper and piñon, the air thin and transparent, and the views from the summit utterly unspoiled. Hard to believe Albuquerque had once looked so clean and small, and in my lifetime, too. Jack Burns wouldn't recognize the sprawling megalopolis Albuquerque has become. He'd probably be glad that a truck had run him and his horse down on the highway at the film's conclusion.

I had a few hours to kill before my meeting with the novelist Max Evans. So I spent them in Old Town, what was once Albuquerque's original *villa*. It was very touristy, but enjoyable nonetheless. I strolled through the Old Town Plaza under centuries-old historic buildings with graceful adobe architecture. I found a gallery that sold outstanding Anasazi and modern Pueblo pottery, the real thing, pottery for the seasoned collector and serious buyer, which I wasn't. I came across R. C. Gorman's gallery and spent some time there looking at paintings and lithographs of his El Greco–like women. At a restaurant called La Hacienda, I ate some chiles rellenos, mild green chiles stuffed with cheese, batter-fried, and topped with a piquant but earthy green sauce. The old adobe restaurant was adorned with fireplaces, *bancos,* and vigas, but it struck me as a tourist trap. The food was bland compared to what I had been eating. I guess not all New Mexican chiles are created equal. I found an antique gunshop that sold swords and Spanish armor, Colt Peacemakers and eighteenth-century dueling pistols. There was a place offering Navajo rugs, Indian pawn, and kachinas, and another selling an eye-watering assortment of New Mexican chile peppers and powders. Max Evans lives on Ridgecrest Drive, a modest middle-class neighborhood in Albuquerque. His house is half-hidden under shade trees. Max told me he liked walking around in the mini-wilderness he had created in his suburban backyard, allowing nature's energies to pour through him. "I walk out there in my backyard, where I make my stories, or, more accurately, where I feel them," Max said.

Max is a cowboy mystic. By age eleven, he was roping calves and having visions. "When I was nine years old," Max said, "I got kicked out of school down in southeastern New Mexico and I had to go over to West Texas and spend a year with my grandmother. She was a spiritualist, a powerful, wonderful, warm person. I studied her and listened to her, and the next thing I knew, I was wide open. By the time I was ten, I started having what they call, facetiously, "supernatural experiences," but they're actually natural. They've never stopped, but they've slowed down some."

Evans is the author of such tough-minded contemporary Westerns as *The Rounders* and *The Hi Lo Country*. He also wrote a sprawling, comic novel about man's relationship and responsibility to the earth, *Bluefeather Fellini*. There hadn't been anything quite like it in contemporary American fiction. It was as if Louis L'Amour had written *One Hundred Years of Solitude*. His eight-hundred-page novel, a real doorstop, tells the story of Bluefeather Fellini, half Italian, half Taos Indian, who walks in two worlds, that of contemporary New Mexico and—for want of a better term—the spiritual plane.

"People didn't quite know what to make of *Bluefeather Fellini*," Max told me. "I don't know how to say this without making it sound like some dumb, damn bragging, but I know it's a great book, and I'm just so damned happy to have lived long enough to have had all those experiences that enabled me to write that book. I was truly blessed."

Max invited me into his house. The walls and shelves of his comfortable living room were adorned with high-quality Southwestern art. Things were a little hectic, as Evans was preparing to leave town for a few days. His life had been quite busy recently. At age seventy-three, Evans had just completed what he called his "one and only historical novel," *Faraway Blue,* about Chief Nana, who led a band of Apache warriors, boys mostly, against the buffalo soldiers in the hellish badlands of the Gila Wilderness in southwestern New Mexico. And a movie based on his famous short novel, *The Hi Lo Country,* was finally coming out after a thirty-seven-year struggle to bring it to the screen.

"For years, Sam Peckinpah tried to get that movie made," Max told me. When his short novel was published in 1961, the author and the film director talked about adapting *The Hi Lo Country* to the screen. But Peckinpah could never get the backing he needed from the studios. "The film would be set to go and then Sam would have another of his wars with the studios," Max said. After Peckinpah died, the film slipped into development limbo for many years, until Martin Scorcese (a New York filmmaker, of all people) read it and moved the project forward. *The Hi Lo Country* tells the story of the friendship between two ranch hands, Pete Calder and Big Boy Matson, and the woman they both love, and their struggles to hold on to the old ways in the face of a changing contemporary West. *The Hi Lo Country* came out of Max's own experiences as a cowpuncher.

"I'm very sad about America right now," Max told me. "I'm sad when I realize how little people know about the rural world. How little they know or care about the actual existence of these people and their livelihoods. The backbone and stability of America comes from the rural country, for God sakes. It's the food and the clothing, the very soul of our existence; it's everything we need to exist in our contemporary society. And its just sad to see the ignorance—the dumbing down of this country is just so readily apparent, and is gaining speed at a foreclosure rate."

Max was born in Ropes, Texas, and before his twelfth birthday had come around, he was working on a ranch south of Santa Fe. Barely out of his teens, he took ownership of a ranch in northeastern New Mexico, a region he would later come to call the Hi Lo Country in his writing. When World War II erupted, Evans made the switch from rancher to combat infantryman. He stormed Omaha Beach on D day. He survived three more bloody campaigns in France and Germany. At the end of the war, Max returned to his New Mexican ranch, but he sold it shortly thereafter so he could move to Taos to become, of all things, a painter. It was there he met his artist wife, Pat James, and the man who was to become his best friend and business partner, Woody Crumbo, a pioneer Potawatami Indian artist, medicine man, and art instructor.

"Woody Crumbo was my artistic and spiritual mentor," Max said. "He was a deeply spiritual man." By the time Max met the artist, Crumbo had made a radical transformation from being a highly popular graphic painter of traditional Native American Indian scenes to an astonishing stylist whose visions seemed to be coming out of some kind of mystical experience. This pioneering shift from watercolors to oils was misunderstood at first, and Crumbo was resented for it. "He had been painting in the Indian graphic style," Max said, "and all of a sudden he decided he would paint these huge pictures, and he pounded on the oil paint in a certain way so that it glowed like jewels. You won't see this in photos of the paintings; you have to see the actual paintings themselves. And by his efforts and sacrifice, he opened up the field for all Indians. And now Indians—artists like R. C. Gorman—can paint any way they please."

Max said he ran into Crumbo at the perfect time. Crumbo was forty and already had some five hundred paintings in museums. He had taught as an instructor at the University of Oklahoma and at the University of Kansas in Wichita. "I became his sole pupil, and later he was my partner in the mining business. It changed me. Already, I was in the spiritual world, but without him, not in a million years would I have been able to do the things I have done."

Evans began painting, and his watercolors and oils, as many as three hundred over time, began to find their way into the hands of public and private collectors. But just as his art career was taking off, Evans decided he wanted to become a writer. So he turned to the typewriter.

He almost didn't survive the transition. To earn money, Evans became a horse trader and also swapped land, automobiles, and antiques for a living. And then he got the idea to prospect for gold, uranium, and other minerals. He and Crumbo went into the mining business together. This wasn't a romance or some fantasy out of *The Treasure of the Sierra Madre*. These were working mines. One mine the two men developed in northern New Mexico produced for over forty years. Neither man became rich, but they made a living. All the while, Evans was writing novels and nonfiction works, publishing in the pulps as well as in serious literary journals.

Evans was to distill his experiences—ranching, combat, gold hunting, his feelings for the mystical—into his great novel of the Southwest, *Bluefeather Fellini*. I wanted to talk to him about the genesis of that book, which interested me more than almost any other novel that had come out of this part of America.

"I tell you, old pardner, I almost gave up on that book. I

started making notes for it around 1950—that's how far back it went. Hundreds and hundreds of notes, written on bar napkins, grocery sacks, every kind of piece of paper imaginable. I took notes all those years. I spent a total of thirty-six years on that book. It took me five and a half years of those thirty-six years to write it."

When he finally thought he might have such a novel in him, "when I thought I might be capable of writing it well enough," Evans gathered up all the notes and scraps of paper and found, to his horror, that he had a twenty-thousand-page pile in front of him.

"Oh God, it was daunting. I had enough for forty short books or twenty long ones. I had to figure out a way to condense it all down into one novel. It almost deserted me. And then I remembered I had written a little story called "Sky of Gold." It was a little story with some cockeyed, original material in it. And so I read it again, and I'll be damned, it was pretty good. And there was my miniature outline for the whole damn book. Within a day, I made up my mind to do the book."

His finished manuscript came in at about a thousand typewritten pages. He couldn't find a publisher. "I really thought I might die before it was published," he said. And then the University Press of Colorado decided, rather bravely, to take it on as its first-ever fictional offering.

"It was a very dangerous thing for them to do and I really appreciated their courage. But they didn't think they could sell a book that big." So *Bluefeather Fellini* was published as two novels, *Bluefeather Fellini* (1993) and *Bluefeather Fellini in the Sacred Realm* (1994). "We went through three editions. And then the Quality Paperback Book Club came out, and we got three more editions there." Bantam also published a pair of massmarket paperbacks. "It's still selling slowly in the hardback UPC edition," he said.

Bluefeather Fellini is the work of a visionary whose vision is reality, a novel about understanding the earth and man's relationship and obligation to it. He said the spirit of his mentor, Woody Crumbo, lives in every chapter. The book's title and the character's name were inspired by the films of one of his favorite directors, Federico Fellini. Evans had difficulty finding a popular market for his novel. The literary establishment tended to dismiss him as a writer of Westerns. Those looking for a Zane Grey experience were baffled by the magical realism.

Ever since he was a young child, Evans said, he had felt the presence of a power—a force, an energy—in the world around him. *Bluefeather Fellini* chronicles the picaresque adventures of a young man whose wild adventures and comic escapades in many ways parallel the author's own life and journey of self-discovery. It is a miraculous life voyage that takes Bluefeather, a truly blessed man, to use Evans's phrase, across the baking deserts of the Southwest and into the bloody battlefields of Europe and back again. When he finally finds the hidden river of gold under the earth, Bluefeather walks away from its vast wealth, choosing instead the real treasure that is all around us and free for the taking.

"Sam Peckinpah was a mystic," Max told me. "Brian Keith was a mystic. Slim Pickens was a mystic. Yes, Slim Pickens—the same one who rode Stanley Kubrick's bomb into eternity, yelling exultantly all the way—few people knew that about him. He was a highly sophisticated, deeply spiritual man." I asked Evans what he meant when he used the word *mystic,* and Evans laughed and said, "I just use that word because I don't have any other that people can understand.

"There's no real word to describe the complexity or the spirituality between man and the plants and animals and the inner earth and the entirety and magnificence of the universe. There is no word. But you know it's there—it's a simple spiritual fact;

it's a physical fact. After you go through these experiences, it becomes natural to you. It becomes so natural in time, that you just keep expecting everyone else to be as open about it. But most people don't admit it. Some people have a great fear of it. People find themselves caught up in the immediacy of finance or powerful struggles of influence—all the crazy things we are susceptible to—and they completely close down and deny the very essence of their being. And that's the saddest thing of all."

I asked Max how these transcendent moments affected his writing. I wanted him to give me a more concrete example of what he meant by *mystical.*

"Well, now I'm going to look like a damn idiot," he said, laughing. "It will embarrass me. I was writing the book *Faraway Blue.* There was so little history on Nana, the great Apache, the greatest warrior who ever lived. Even less on the Medal of Honor–winning buffalo soldier Moses Williams. So I got a retired general to do all the research he could into the military history of Moses Williams. And I traveled out there and went over all that land where the two men had their great battles. So I had enough for a story, but I wanted to reach beyond what history had recorded.

"It was late November. I was stalled on Nana. I had run out of research. I went out into my backyard. And all of a sudden, a golden butterfly floated over the top of my head and circled in the sky and came back over my head again. Now it's November—it breaks all the rules of nature and science for a butterfly to be out there at that time of year. But the butterfly was there, and then it disappeared into a sacred hole in the sky— call it the sky door—that I've experienced before. A great thrill came over me and I sat down at my typewriter, and I had a full chapter—I was just guided by that man's spirit. I don't question it or anything.

"The butterfly stayed in my backyard all throughout the winter. It would come two or three times a week. Toward March, I was getting closer to finishing the book. And I got to the point where I could make prayers and the butterfly would show up.

"And one day, I turned to my wife, Pat, and asked her if she saw the butterfly. And she told me, 'I've been watching that butterfly fly over your head out the back of the kitchen window all winter.'

"Now, I know this makes an idiot out of me in the eyes of most of the world. But I don't care, because it's the truth. What's in that book came to me from a source beyond recorded history. It guided me and helped me. I had the same experience with *The One-Eyed Sky*. *Faraway Blue*—I never could have done that book without this so-called spiritual world, or whatever the hell you want to call it."

21

SPIRIT COUNTRY

I LEFT MAX Evans pondering his sacred hole in the sky. People everywhere, in every culture, have felt some kind of emanation of the divine, and often these feelings are tied to nature. Darwin suspected that mankind's feelings of awe for what we have come to think of as God or the spiritual arose from some feature of our neurological makeup. God resides in our neural fire, so to speak. Perhaps this circuitry evolved within the human species as a means of coping with the foreknowledge of death, an insight other animals probably weren't burdened with. Some geneticists now believe there might even be a "religion" gene. If this is so, then conceivably that gene could be isolated or even removed entirely from the human species, and mankind would lose its sense of the sacred. (And if God wasn't already dead, man could finish him off.)

I suppose if one has to have a religion, a rather vaguely defined nature pantheism would fit the bill for me. Call it "the religion before religion." There is a sense that the creation is still going on moment by moment, that the world is creating itself every nanosecond. That the cosmic music is still being written. And that not a single act in this creative pageant has been planned. Here in the Western world, man has come up with the idea that he was created in the image of God. I suspect this is true only so far as our spinning atoms are concerned.

What puzzles me is the difference between those of us who are susceptible to these feelings about nature and those people who just can't feel anything about it at all. I don't know what those differences are—psychological perhaps. The real fascination about nature has something to do with the bigger picture, the entirety of life itself. These experiences have given us access to our true selves. I think they are essential to our well-being, our vitality. I would go so far as to say that these feelings are a part of our biological inheritance. But our inheritance, like the entirety of the planet, has been put up for sale. Our birthright is being converted into cash. You can see this on the outskirts of places like Albuquerque and Santa Fe. You can see it in Las Vegas. You can see it in the smog drifting over the Grand Canyon.

From Albuquerque, I made several futile attempts to phone the Havasupai Indian Reservation down in the Grand Canyon to see if I could reserve a campsite at Havasu. My road trip was nearing its end. I wanted to finish my sojourn by floating in Havasu Canyon's turquoise waters, as I had done eleven years ago. I was going to be passing close by the Grand Canyon's South Rim on my way back home and I felt Havasu would be as fitting a place as any to end this trip. But there was no answer at Havasupai Tourist Enterprise. They are notorious for not answering their phones, especially during the high season, when they are flooded with reservations. And the campground in Havasu Canyon had probably been booked up for months in advance. I could spend all day on the phone and might never get through. And so I abandoned my plan. Havasu

Canyon would have to wait for another time. But that was all right; I was tired and satisfied and ready to go home.

I don't know exactly what I was meant to find on my brief road trip. But I suspected I had found it, whatever it was. There's no denying the mystique of the place. The Southwest is a bit of everything. It's a landscape so primal, it could stand for the entirety of the planet, the wet regions as well as the dry ones. I had obviously become fixed on the desert at a very active and deep level in my psyche.

Of all the places I had been privileged to visit on my jaunt, I wasn't at all surprised that the ones that ended up meaning the most to me, the Escalante region and Canyonlands, were precisely those places still the closest to being true wildernesses. I had already decided that the next time I came out here, I would spend more time roughing it in the Escalante, in its backcountry, away from the roadside campgrounds. And I'd explore the remote Maze area in Canyonlands, which I had yet to experience firsthand. And I'd hike all the way out to Point Sublime on the North Rim of the Grand Canyon and lose myself there. The wilder something is, the more real it becomes. We know that in our bones. We need the wild as much as we need civilization. That is why it hurts so much to see these wild places polluted and spoiled. It is a vandalism not just against nature but a form of violence against ourselves. The sense of there being something absolutely sacred and unspoiled out there is a big part of what it means to be a human being.

I DROVE INTO the setting sun, bound for Gallup, New Mexico, into the badlands, the checkerboard lands of the Navajo Nation. I found myself crossing desolate vistas under the forbidding Zuni Buttes. The glare of the setting sun in my windshield blinded me. Speeding trucks almost ran me off the interstate. The countryside was—well, not lovely.

Gallup, New Mexico, on a Friday night. I rolled into town an hour after sundown. The weekend was just starting. I could feel the excitement building. Gallup is said to be the most Indian of all off-reservation towns. I didn't hear any drums throbbing in the night, but pickups full of Navajo prowled the town. The honky-tonk barrooms were filling up. Route 66, the famous roadway whose song inspired us to get our kicks on it, ran down the center of Gallup, paralleling the newer interstate. I drove by budget motels, convenience stores, and gas stations and heard the evening train rolling through town. I rented a room and picked up food and beverage at a convenience store. I had given up drinking a few years back, so I wasn't going to see Gallup bar life.

Back in my motel room, restless, bored with what was on TV, I decided to get back into my car and drive out into the darkness on the edge of the desert. This was to be my last night in the Southwest. In another day, I would be back home in San Francisco. I wanted to see the diamond constellations over the high desert one last time. The night was absolutely clear. I found a dirt road leading off the highway and drove for some miles, until the lights of Gallup were so far behind me that they meant nothing.

I parked my car on the side of the dirt track and got out. There was only elemental darkness and desert and a sky lit with stars. From where I stood, at this high altitude, without the distraction of ambient city light, I could see what must have been every single star that is visible to the naked eye from this spot on earth, at this time of night, in the June heavens. But what struck me was not so much the number of stars as the empty space between them. I looked up and found archers and insects, swans and bears, winged horses and water dippers. I wondered what names the Navajo had given these star designs.

What a miracle existence is. How fortunate we are to experience it. Statistically speaking, the mere probability of any of us being here at all is so infinitesimal, it is laughable. Try to imagine the eons that passed before you came into being. Now try and imagine the eternity that will come after you are gone. For the briefest moment in the span of eternity, we have the amazing good luck to exist. Now what were the odds of that happening? Think of spermatozoa as being more numerous than all the stars visible up there. Each of us comes from a single sperm that has managed to break into and fertilize a single egg. In just one orgasm, upward of 25 million sperm are ejaculated. Each sperm cell contains the basis, the raw material, of something, someone totally unique. And to think that on the night of your conception, only one sperm cell outraced all the others to make that journey all the way to its conclusion and succeed in fertilizing your mother's egg. The one and only sperm cell that was the seed of your consciousness. The one sperm and egg combination that could go toward making that unique human being that is you. Had another of those millions of sperm beat it to the finish line, you wouldn't have come into existence at all. Another human being, another uniquely formed individual, with a separate state of consciousness, would have won the lottery of life. Now think of the number of sperm produced by a single male human, your father, over a lifetime. Imagine all those random ejaculations. And now consider this: Each one of us comes from a long and uninterrupted line of male and female human beings going back to the dawn of mankind—and before that to animals, and before that to lesser living organisms—who somehow, on a planet filled with unbelievable obstacles and dangers, managed to survive long enough to divide and evolve, breed and give birth. What a miraculous privilege it is to stand in this desert and stare up at the constellations and to know that things, *things,* actually exist. And that there is such a thing as *consciousness.* To know that there are wonders out there like the Grand Canyon and the Colorado River and that you are alive and living in a time when you can see them. Who among us has the right even to complain or be unhappy?

Well, perhaps we do have that right. We know that someday we will have to give all this up and cease to exist. Men must endure their going hence, even as their coming hither, wrote Shakespeare in *King Lear*. We disappear practically in the moment of our becoming. We are probably the only animals on the planet who realize this. That is the special burden of being human. Somewhere on the savannas of eastern Africa it happened—the first creature was born, separated from the rest of the cosmos. Separated by a capacity for rational thought. Separated from earth by its straining for heaven. And free, free to choose. A new beauty was added to the splendor of the universe that day on the green savannas of Africa. But could so much as a single particle of that new human consciousness survive death? Not bloody likely, I'd say. Life is a bird that flies out of the darkness into a lighted room and then flies back out into the darkness again. So said the Venerable Bede, a medieval ecclesiastic who never saw the Grand Canyon, never saw the desert stars over New Mexico. It's an unnerving thought, oblivion—to be flying back into a night as dark as the inside of a crow. No awareness, no retention, nada. No more physical and material reality. Life is a comedy to those who think, a tragedy to those who feel. Who said that? Everett Ruess? Edward Abbey? The *Albuquerque Journal*? Perhaps it is writ large on those pictographs on the Great Gallery of Horseshoe Canyon.

Still, I'll take it. And I'll take the times we were born into, as well. I may resent the encroachment of the machine into the garden, but I also appreciate electric light and ice cubes. *Homo sapiens* have spent most of the last 100,000 years of human existence squatting in caves. It has only been in the last eight generational lifetimes (given the biblical three score and ten as man's allotted life span) that humankind has even seen the printed word. And only one lifetime for the moving picture. And only half a lifetime for television, sweet television. And we go back a million years!

I drove back to Gallup to watch a moving picture on a television screen that was bolted onto a stand in my motel room. It was *The Searchers,* John Ford's classic Western, filmed at Monument Valley. And it was pretty good entertainment, too. When you think about it, we really don't watch enough television. I suspect that when the end comes at last and we are lying on our deathbeds, our big regret will be that we didn't watch quite enough TV while we had the chance.

SUNRISE. I AWOKE to an unblemished desert. Looking westward, I saw the Painted Cliffs and distant ranges I would have to cross. My route would take me out of Gallup in between mountain gaps and low passes. The desert was still cool but wouldn't remain so for long under the blast furnace of the rising sun. I filled the tank and checked the oil. Best to keep the Blazer running smoothly and properly. Get it back to the rental agency in one piece. No air conditioning for me, though; I like the air of the Southwest the way it is, without any conditions.

Shall I describe my drive back through Arizona? I think not. The by-now-familiar red terrain dotted with junipers and piñon. The Painted Desert, petrified forests, and dinosaur beds. Little old men and women poking along in gigantic RVs. Vacationing families traveling by van on the interstate, bumper stickers reading: MY CHILD PASSED THE METAL DETECTOR AT RONALD REAGAN HIGH SCHOOL. MY SON IS ON THE HONOR ROLL AT THE FLAGSTAFF JUVENILE DETENTION CENTER. Bumper stickers and T-shirts are the atheneums of the future. I spot a bumper sticker pasted above a Tennessee license plate: WHEN EVOLU-

TION IS OUTLAWED, ONLY OUTLAWS WILL EVOLVE. Out of the red-and-umber desert into the pine belt of Arizona. The San Francisco Peaks, a conifer haze coming off the national forest. The sky like the bluebird of happiness. An increasing flow of automobile traffic turning off at the junction for the Grand Canyon. The hot fury of the wind whistling at seventy-five miles per hour past my open window.

I was filled with a sense of freedom and joy at being in the country of the western United States. How I loved this land. Not out of any misguided sense of patriotism—after all, I'm not a jingoist or an idiot. I love America because the great deserts and mountains and trout rivers all seem to be out here.

In thirteen hours, I would be in San Francisco. From the high desert to the foghorn bay. One long burst of driving, like a character in a Kerouac novel. I would probably arrive an hour after dusk. I'll see those tongues of flame licking at the night sky above the East Bay refineries. The San Francisco Bay Area would be lit up with grids of electric fire, and it would be like looking into God's brain. No doubt the fog would appear ghostly in the halogen lighting. Crossing San Francisco Bay, I'd be able to make out Fisherman's Wharf seen through a veil of Pacific mist. On foggy nights the bridge spans, with their moving streams of headlights, look like nothing less than strands of pearls strung across the Bay. Wipers ticked time, flashing at condensation where earlier there had been Mojave dust on my windshield. Out there in the darkness beyond the Golden Gate, moaning foghorns were singing cargo ships home from foreign ports.

I would go to sleep that night listening to the foghorns, but the desert would be in my subconscious. In my American West, in the West of my dreaming imagination, there would be little roadside culture, few tourist traps, and not a single river plugged up and ruined by a dam. There would be no Las Vegas to pollute the views of the Grand Canyon. Albuquerque might be wreathed in smog, but in my New Mexico, there would be only the clarity of adobe light. In my dreams, the desert would not yet have paid the awful price for being beautiful.

Glad to be home, but a little regretful, too. Still the desert Southwest will always be there for me to love and return to while I am alive. When you come to the continent's edge, you can always go back and retrace your steps. And the going will be just as good as the coming.

The Southwest is candescent. You can feel yourself being drawn into its heat and light. I feel myself out there now, among the distant blue mesas and red tablelands, watching giant cloud shadows folding into canyons and drifting across the desert. I can hear ravens in the sky and smell the water holes. And when moonlit evening comes, with a perfume of datura on the night air, an arcane magic takes hold. It is the shaman's hour. The desert is tranquil and mysterious and clearly under a spell. And yet I feel a sense of foreboding, as if time is running out, and the Anasazi are hiding in the darkness, watching me and wondering who I am.